THEY HAVE A WORD FOR IT

They Have a *Word* for It

A Lighthearted Lexicon of Untranslatable Words & Phrases

HOWARD RHEINGOLD

Sarabande Books

LOUISVILLE, KENTUCKY

**Reprinted by arrangement with Jeremy Tarcher/
Putnam, a member of Penguin/Putnam Inc.**

LIBRARY OF CONGRESS CATALOGING-IN-PUBLICATION DATA

Rheingold, Howard.
    They have a word for it.
    Bibliography.
    Includes index.
    1. Terms and phrases. 2. Idioms. I. Title.
P305.R48   1988   413'.1   87-17999
ISBN 0-87477-464-0 (pbk.)

THIS EDITION: ISBN 1-889330-46-9 (pbk.)

Cover and text design by Charles Casey Martin.

Manufactured in the United States of America.
This book is printed on acid-free paper.

Sarabande Books is a nonprofit literary organization.

To Judy and Mamie,
who fill my life with light.
Because of you I am a
cuor contento.

TABLE OF CONTENTS

ACKNOWLEDGMENTS

Any mistakes you may find are the responsibility of the author. And any peculiar ideas you might find in the following pages are undoubtedly the author's. But the raw material for this work came from a variety of sources and people. The inspiration for the book, the intellectual and financial support, and the constant, energizing enthusiasm came from Jeremy Tarcher. First among the network of informants, scholars, friends, word-lovers, and meme-collectors who directed my attention to intriguing words was Corinne Hawkins, my researcher. Others who helped in large and small ways were Ramon Sender Barayon, Ari Davidow, Lila Forest, David Gans, Max Knight, Milissa Koloski, Ziggie Koren, Dr. Lew Lancaster, Leo Pruden, Stephanie Rick, Paul Saffo, and Maria Syndicus.

INTRODUCTION
Hearing Is Believing

The Cracks Between Our Worldviews

This book is meant to be fun. Open it at random and see if you don't find something that will amuse you, entertain you, titillate your curiosity, tickle your perspective. But you should know that reading this book might have serious side effects at a deeper level. Even if you read one page as you stand in a bookstore, you are likely to find a custom or an idea that could change the way you think about the world. It has to do with the insidious way words mold thoughts.

It all started with a friendly lunch. Jeremy Tarcher is the kind of publisher a writer dreams about. He isn't likely to merge with a new multinational conglomerate every other week, as book publishers are wont to do, and he actually likes to sit down with authors and talk about ideas. During one of our brainstorming sessions, Jeremy mentioned his desire to publish a lexicon of "untranslatable words" that don't exist in English but would add a new dimension to our lives if we were somehow to import them from their original languages. Words that would open a window on the way other cultures encourage people to think and feel, and thus point out new ways for us to think and feel.

"Oh, you mean words like *wabi*," I said.

"Perhaps," he replied. "What does it mean?"

"It's a Japanese concept for a certain kind of beauty," I explained. "It means a lot of things, but most Japanese people know *wabi* when they see it. In general, it means a kind of rough spontaneity, of the kind you might see in a rustic raku pot or some minimalist calligraphy by an old master. I like to contrast it to the kind of studied perfection often valued in the West: high-rises, photorealism—all the shiny, perfect stuff that looks like it could have been produced by a machine."

"Yes, that is what I mean," he agreed. But neither one of us was quite sure how to proceed, or whether there were that many words out there. So I called on a friend who is an expert on various Asian languages. Did he think there were enough examples for a book on untranslatable words?

"Oh, you mean words like *ho'oponopono*," he replied.

"Perhaps," I said. "What does it mean?"

"It's a Hawaiian word for a kind of social therapy with religious overtones. Everybody involved in a dispute goes into a room and vows to stay there until they talk it all out."

While my friend the language expert convinced me that there are indeed many foreign-language words for concepts unfamiliar or unknown in English, he wasn't a great deal of help in tracking down more of them. In the long run, I found that just about everybody who knows a foreign language knows an untranslatable word. My friend Maria, who was brought up in Germany, told me about *Torschlüsspanik* (now in chapter three, "Dance of the Sexes"), the frantic anxiety experienced by unmarried women as they race against the "biological clock." When I went to a panel meeting and the fellow sitting next to me asked what I was doing lately, I told him about my quest for untranslatable words. He turned out to be an amateur Mayan scholar, and he pointed me toward the remarkable uses the Mayans make of *bol*, their word for "in-law" (see chapter one, "Human Family Affairs").

I've never had so much fun gathering information for a book. After friends and acquaintances had contributed their one or two gems, I found that the anthropological literature was a rich source of material. I even used a computer bulletin board to gather tips, and through it I met Corinne, my researcher, who extended my list of a couple of dozen words to a list of several hundred, from which I selected the entries for this book.

For those of you who haven't dipped into the world of cybernetic virtual communities, a computer bulletin board is a computer that is hooked up to a telephone line. People who know that computer's telephone number can use their own computer to dial in to the bulletin board, then look through a menulike list of conversations that are stored in the bulletin board system (known in the acronym-happy computer world as a "BBS"), in order to find a topic of discussion that interests them. Then they can add their own words to the discussion by typing messages on their home computers, which transmit the words to the BBS for

others to read. When I started researching this book, I
posted an announcement on my local BBS, proclaiming
that I would buy dinner for contributors of new and interesting untranslatable words. Some of my best tips were har-
vested from this BBS, which also yielded some of my best
new friendships.

Thinking about the right kind of untranslatable words
creates a certain state of mind. I found myself looking at the
mundane elements of everyday life through a new kind of
lens, which revealed to me dimensions in my familiar environment that I simply had not seen before because I hadn't
known how to look. That is precisely where the magic of
naming the world, as first practiced by Adam in the Garden of Eden, can exert a subtle leverage. Finding a name for
something is a way of conjuring its existence, of making it
possible for people to see a pattern where they didn't see
anything before. I gradually came to realize that the collective human worldview is far larger than any one of our individual languages leads us to believe. After sifting through all
the strange, delightful, horrifying, and hilarious things that
people use special words to name, I became sympathetic to
the idea that we think and behave the way we do in large
part because we have words that make these thoughts and
behaviors possible, acceptable, and useful.

I am not a linguist, and this book is not an attempt to
provide rigorous evidence for one linguistic hypothesis or
another. But when I did some reading about the linguistic
theory known as the Whorfian hypothesis, I began to understand the formal underpinnings of the phenomenon I had

come to know through sheer iteration of examples. In light of these theories about the influence of thought upon language, I began to see this book as something quite different from the other books about unusual words. Although it is great fun to read about strange and curious words, unless those words also happen to match semantic niches in our culture—a real social need for a specific attitude, object, or behavior—they are no more than amusements. But a book of *useful*, heretofore untranslated words for attitudes, objects, or behaviors that we don't have but might need in America could become something more powerful than an amusement. It could become an instrument of change.

If you want to change the way people think, you can educate them, brainwash them, bribe them, drug them. Or you can teach them a few carefully chosen new words. I believe that the memes and messages conveyed by the entries in these pages have the power to change the way you see the world (or, as the Germans would say, these words might warp your *Weltanschauung*). Ultimately, I believe the foreign words collected and discussed here have the potential for transforming the way our entire culture sees the world. This mind-altering and culture-shifting side effect of adopting untranslatable words from other languages stems from a phenomenon linguists call "linguistic relativity." The following passage conveys the essence of that theory:

> We dissect nature along lines laid down by our native languages. The categories and types that we isolate from the world of phenomena we do not find there because they stare every observer in the face; on the contrary, the world is presented in a kaleidoscopic flux of impressions which has to be organized by

our minds—and this means largely by the linguistic systems in our minds. We cut nature up, organize it into concepts, and ascribe significances as we do, largely because we are parties to an agreement to organize it this way—an agreement that holds throughout our speech community and is codified in the patterns of our language.

The words quoted above were written by Benjamin Lee Whorf, an expert on American Indian languages. This passage from *Language, Thought and Reality* is the heart of the theory that has come to be known as the Whorfian hypothesis, which asserts that the world is experienced in different ways by different linguistic communities and proposes that the differences in language actually *cause* the differences in the way linguistic communities think. In other words, Whorf claims that language is not just a neutral vessel for conveying thoughts but is an invisible mold that actually shapes the way people think and perceive.

Decades of psychological and anthropological research have failed to prove or disprove the Whorfian hypothesis, although several provocative experiments have demonstrated a strong influence, if not a rigid determination, exerted by language on the way people think. In one of the key experiments, two investigators, Brown and Lenneberg, looked at the effects of language on the ability to discriminate colors. Are colors an objective correlate of phenomena in the external world? Or are they influenced by what we think and believe, by the words we speak? If you have no words for green, for example, is it more difficult to discriminate between a green card and a blue one? Brown and Lenneberg chose subjects for an experiment from cultures that had different words, or no words at all, for particular colors, and tested their color memory abilities in various ways. Those subjects who already had a name for a color tended to discriminate more quickly between two similar colors than those subjects who had no name for that color.

More provocative and far more entertaining than all the carefully controlled experiments are the "untranslatable" words that seem to support the Whorfian hypothesis simply by existing. When you learn enough about the Japanese concept of *wabi* (chapter four, "The Eye of the Beholder"), your own concept of beauty will never be exactly the same. A brief glimpse at a Hawaiian *ho'oponopono* (chapter one, "Human Family Affairs") will alter your opinions on domestic disputes. And an understanding of the Haida *potlatch* (chapter five, "Serious Business") might reverse the way you think about sensible economic behavior.

My reading also revealed that words are capable of influencing events in the external world because of the way they affect our judgment. I discovered that Whorf did not start out as an investigator of language, but as an investigator of the cause of *fires*! Working for an insurance company before he undertook his extensive study of American Indian languages, Whorf discovered that the way people misunderstood certain words was the cause of many fires. The chief culprit was the word *empty*: People would exercise caution near barrels that were full of flammable liquid but all too often did not hesitate to toss matches into "empty" gasoline drums (which were filled with flammable fumes).

As I looked at the way people around me used words, and

as I began to survey the anthropological and linguistic literature, I realized that certain words act like linguistic viruses;
patterns of meaning seem to propagate themselves throughout linguistic communities via mysterious, unofficial, ad hoc
channels because a semantic niche in that community is cry-
ing out for a precise word. English is a hodgepodge of such
words that have found their way into the language. When
enough time passes, Hindi words like *pajama* or French
words like *elite* simply become acceptable in English. Sometimes, foreign words that mean one thing become English
words that fit a definition that didn't exist when the foreign word evolved: *hospice*, for example, was originally a
French word for inns set up for travelers by various monas-
tic orders; the word recently has been adopted in English
for a place where people can die in peace and dignity.

There is an intermediate category, a kind of linguistic
waiting room, consisting of words like *déjà vu* (the French
word for the feeling that one has experienced something
before) or *siesta* (the Spanish word for a midday nap) that are
widely used in English but are still considered to be "foreign."
I was looking for words that weren't yet part of the language
(or queued up in the English-language waiting room) and
that described concepts that might enrich our own worldview,
or at least offer us insight into the ways our language can
restrict the way we think about ourselves and the world. And
that is the not-so-hidden agenda of this project: to make visible
that which was previously unnoticed, to help us to see new
characteristics and possibilities in ourselves, our friends, our
coworkers. We all inherit a worldview along with our native

language. Untranslatable words help us notice the cracks between our own worldview and those of others.

My intention was not to conduct an exhaustive scientific search, and the result is not intended as a contribution to the rigorous science of linguistics. And although I respect the need for formal, systematic study of language, I have never strayed too far from the idea that languages are living systems and are shaped by people who use words, not by linguists who study them. Every word that came from the linguistic or anthropological literature has been presented in terms that nonspecialists will understand or appreciate, and if some of the precision of the strict definition has been lost in one case or another, the fault is mine. I attempted to verify every word that was suggested by a native speaker of a foreign language or by a person who had collected an interesting word during his or her travels, but if an occasional definition strays slightly from the orthodox lexicon, the fault is my own.

In the overwhelming majority of these entries, however, you will find that the word means exactly what I have said it means—if you make allowances for the fact that a concept native to, say, the Southeast Asian highlands had to be described in terms that a Southern California suburbanite could grasp.

If the more familiar Romance languages seem underrepresented, and the esoteric languages like Bantu, Kiriwana, or Navajo offered in abundance, it is because some people from obscure linguistic groups have come up with words that represent powerful ideas. If a word from a group of islands in the Indian Ocean conveys an idea that would be just as significant in Los Angeles or Minneapolis, I included it. There is a sprinkling of Italian, an abundant pinch of German, a soupçon of French, a bit of Yiddish, a generous helping of Japanese and Chinese in these pages, along with tidbits of Sanskrit, Tibetan, Indonesian, Iroquois, Tierra del Fuegan, Pascuense (language of the Easter Islands), Scottish, Bantu, and a half dozen truly obscure languages. The sophisticated linguist will recognize as many as a dozen words. In fact, if you can recognize a dozen words, that's proof positive that you are a sophisticated linguist. And if you can use them in conversation, consider yourself an *accomplished* sophisticated linguist.

This book differs from other amusing and intriguing collections of unusual words because *these words are meant to be used.* Some will make you see things differently, many will help you show others how to see in new ways. Don't worry about strict pronunciation. Go ahead and make these words an active part of your vocabulary. It is unlikely that a Kiriwina-speaking Trobriand islander will jump into your conversation to correct you. And if a person fluent in Navajo catches you in a slight mispronunciation, appreciation of your efforts will surely outweigh any reproach for your accent. Don't let the fear of criticism by the bores and *Korinthenkackers* (chapter five) affect you. You will find a confident power well up when you muster the courage to help expand the scope of our language.

As entries began to accumulate, I noticed that they grouped themselves into various categories: words about human family relations, business, technology, the dance of the sexes, beauty and aesthetics, dreams, spirituality, politics, states of mind, words about words, and words that captured my interest but didn't seem to fit into one category or another (and which I ended up calling "Strange Memes"). After the words were sorted into these semantic bins, I realized that a strict alphabetic order wasn't aesthetically pleasing, so Jeremy and I shuffled and reshuffled the order until it became a series of intuitive, evocative juxtapositions. You can read the book in any order, either front-to-back serial order or random-access style. In some cases, a word in one category or language is related in an intriguing way to a word in another category or language, and these linkages are duly noted; you can follow these chains of semantic association if you like, as a third alternative route through the book.

On the matter of pronunciation, I avoided the various typographical systems for conveying precise pronunciation. Most people aren't sure how to interpret an upside-down "e" or the various accents and subscripts that linguists and lexicographers use. So I stuck with a less formal way of breaking down foreign syllables into English words or sounds, sometimes augmenting those with "rhymes with" constructions. For those words I found too interesting to exclude from the book despite there being no exact pronunciation available, I have suggested a pronunciation anyway. In the case of languages like Chinese, where intonation is important, it is nearly impossible to convey exact pronunciation. English speakers tend to have difficulty with foreign accents, and if we are to adopt exotic words for our usage, it's the meaning that counts. By the time enough of us use these words, they won't be foreign. And the accepted pronunciation will be the one used by the largest number of people.

When works of science or literature by another author have been cited in this book, the full reference to the original has been listed in the Bibliography. A brief Key to Sources/Index is also included, with a list of pointers to items in the Bibliography. Feel free to use this Index as a navigational tool for your own semantic explorations. If a particular word fascinates you, look it up in the Index; then consult the Bibliography to find a reference to a book or article that can tell you more. Perhaps you will discover, as I did, that one word leads to another, and that something as small and apparently insignificant as an unusual word from a foreign language can lead you on a wonderful treasure hunt through the world of ideas.

CHAPTER ONE

Human Family Affairs

People Words

We do not talk only in order to reason or to inform. We have to make love and quarrel, to propitiate and pardon, to rebuke, console, intercede, and arouse. "He that complains," said Johnson, "acts like a man, like a social being."

> C. S. Lewis, *At the Fringe of Language*

Human beings... are very much at the mercy of the particular language which has become the medium of expression for their society.... The fact of the matter is that the "real world" is, to a large extent, unconsciously built up on the language habits of the group.... We see and hear and otherwise experience very largely as we do because the language habits of our community predispose certain choices of interpretation.

> Edward Sapir, *The Relation of Habitual Thought and Behavior to Language*

Everybody has a mother, and most people have in-laws, but anthropologists have discovered that there are nearly as many ways of reckoning kinship as there are cultures on the planet. The esteem, or lack of it, with which people regard their relatives and neighbors varies widely from culture to culture and is often reflected in the vocabularies people use to describe their relationships. To the Apaches, who live in a harsh desert environment, in-laws are called *sitike*, and the relationship involves a kind of sacred obligation. To the Mayans, who live in an abundant tropical environment, the word *bol* is used as the noun for "in-law" and as an extraordinarily pejorative adjective.

The kinds of social arrangements to be found in different cultures vary as widely as their kinship systems. You don't have to be kin to have complex relationships—neighbors and friends are also objects of affection and scorn. The kinds of problems people have with one another, as well as the cultural mechanisms we have for dealing with these problems, are reflected in our vocabularies. In Hawaii, people deal with domestic disputes by arranging a *ho'oponopono*. On Easter Island, the words *hakamaroo* and *tingo* refer to different kinds of outrageous borrowing behavior. The Yiddish words *tsuris* and *nakhes* refer to two extreme emotions that only your son or daughter can invoke in you.

Social games can be methods for disarming potentially explosive conflicts, as the Pascuense words *anga-anga*, *hakanuka-nuka*, and *ngaobera* attest. Words can evoke a sentimental dream, like the German term *gemütlich*. In Bali, a society where people are very closely involved with one another, the word *ramé* describes something at once chaotic and joyful. And Indonesians use the word *rojong* to describe a natural and guileless kind of human relationship that ought to be included in every human culture.

Social relationships are not always harmonious, and some terms are not always complimentary: The German *fisselig* describes something you don't want to happen to you; the Scottish *suilk* refers to something you definitely don't want to be caught doing at the dinner table; the French phrase *épater les bourgeois* describes a category of behavior that has induced physical nausea in middle-class parents for countless generations.

Other words describe social contracts that aren't familiar in our culture...yet: The Polish *dozywocie* is a parental contract that might or might not work here; the Spanish *confianza* is reserved for a human relationship more unshakable and profound than that of a mere "good friend." Some words describe joyous social behaviors, as in the Bantu term *mbuki-mvuki*, which involves shucking off all clothing for party purposes. And other words, like the German *Zeitgeist*, describe cultural abstractions that convey the quintessentials of human social behavior.

Words about families, social groups, and human relationships have the most intimate kind of power. As we witness the emergence of a society where family relationships are changing in profound ways (intermarriage and single parents are two prominent examples), we need words to help us reinvent the family. Just as we could make fantastic progress with new technologies, new ways of doing business, and new states of mind by learning the appropriate word-magic for each endeavor, we can make astonishing progress with one another by picking up a few important new words.

Words are the glue that keeps social groups together or stirs them up. The right word can salve a misunderstanding or provoke a riot. With all the complexity and importance of human family affairs, it pays to have a few new words to describe those situations that just aren't covered by the orthodox lexicon. Every culture seems to have its own way of dealing with friendship, love, in-laws, strangers, siblings. Some cultures have come up with words that can actually create new kinds of relationships. Here they are. Use them. Teach them to your friends and family. See if your family life doesn't manifest an added dimension of clarity and felicity.

ho'oponopono (Hawaiian)
Solving a problem by talking it out. [noun]

We don't have this social mechanism in our culture, but we could well use it. A *ho'oponopono* (HO-OH-poh-no-poh-no) is *a social gathering and healing process that combines the functions of a religious ceremony, group therapy, family counseling session, town-hall meeting, and small-claims court.* An occasion for a *ho'oponopono* might be a dispute between in-laws, a disagreement between business partners, sexual complications, or minor territorial disagreements. After an invocation of the gods, the aggrieved parties sit down and discuss the issue until it is set right (the Hawaiian root word *pono* means "righteousness"). The closest analogy in the West comes from the realm of labor management relations, where "locked-door arbitration" is sometimes used to resolve disputes. The principle is the same: Everybody agrees to stay in the same room until some resolution is reached.

In North America, because we are such a heterogeneous culture, citizens require many different forums for settling disputes and healing human relationships. *Ho'oponopono* originated in Hawaii, where the original native culture was racially, culturally, and religiously homogeneous, so it is not surprising to find that certain Hawaiian words reveal inter-relationships of kinship ties, spiritual duties, and livelihood. In the United States, we might find it easier to settle interpersonal conflicts peacefully and equitably if we were to adopt some words (and corresponding attitudes) from societies like that of ancient Hawaii.

In our socially fragmented, serially monogamous, increasingly litigious society, both weddings and divorces are occasions in which a *ho'oponopono* might be preferable to the currently popular means of conflict resolution. "If your family and my family can't agree on the seating arrangement for our wedding, maybe we ought to round everybody up for a *ho'oponopono*." In this instance, the word would be used as a noun, combining and expanding the meanings of "showdown," "confrontation," "family discussion," and "therapy." But it could be used as a verb of last resort: "That does it. There's nothing left for us to do about this disagreement. We'll have to *ho'oponopono*." Or "Instead of a custody battle, why don't we *ho'oponopono*?" In families and in partnerships, the word could be used to symbolize a powerful covenant—an agreement to attempt to renegotiate crucial relationships whenever they are so out of tune that conflicts arise. As such, *ho'oponopono* could come to mean a new kind of agreement between people who live or work with one another, a verbal symbol of a mutual "arbitration" clause in the unwritten social contracts that bind us into families, communities, and societies.

hakamaroo [noun] and *tingo* [noun/verb] (Pascuense, Easter Island)
Outrageously aggressive or subtly flattering borrowing behavior.

The comic-strip antics of Dagwood Bumstead and his long-suffering neighbor, Herb Woodley, are classic antiheroic themes of American pop mythology. Objects, mostly tools, that Dagwood and Herb borrow from each other and fail to return are the recurrent triggering elements in an endless series of plots that always end up in fist-swinging melees. At this level, the concept of outrageous borrowing as a form of social aggression is well known to most English-speaking people. But we don't have specific words for different kinds of outrageous borrowing. Nor does English have a word for borrowing as a *positive* social act, a subtle form of flattery and homage.

Indeed, in today's mobile American society, the idea of staying in the same place long enough to borrow something from your neighbor has a hint of nostalgia to it. The inhabitants of Easter Island, members of an extremely isolated and geographically immobile society, use the word *hakamaroo* (hah-kah-mahr-OH-oh) to describe *the act of keeping borrowed objects until the owner has to ask for them back.* As Dagwood and Herb know, *hakamaroo* is only the first step on a sophisticated hierarchy of escalating affronts. Psychoanalysts might describe such behavior as "passive-aggressive." And while it might be funny in a comic strip, in real life *hakamaroo* is usually part of a larger, painful pattern of hostility. Putting a name to it might help people resolve or avert this kind of silent aggression: "Herb," a real-life Dagwood might say, "this is the second garden tool you've borrowed this month. And you haven't returned my rake yet. Are you being forgetful? Or is this some kind of *hakamaroo*?"

Borrowing is not always hostile on Easter Island; indeed, it can serve as a kind of social glue. Another Pascuense word, *tingo* (rhymes with "bingo"), carries the concept a step further, into a strange borderland between breach of etiquette and high praise: *Tingo* means *to take all the objects one desires from the house of a friend, one at a time, by asking to borrow them.* The social meaning of this behavior is similar to the Haida word *potlatch*, which refers to an act of giving that confers social status on the gift-giver (see chapter five for more about *potlatch*). If you admire a friend's possession long enough to ask for it, you are paying the donor a supreme compliment; the act of giving it to you is a power exchange that enhances the donor's social status.

Perhaps if we adopted the custom of *tingo* and used the word openly to refer to it, a new awareness of the power of possessions might catch on. The currently popular way of life dedicated to the relentless pursuit of new cars, bigger houses, more powerful appliances—status symbols—followed by the ritual display of these symbolic objects and accompanying symbolic boasting, might grow into some-

thing wonderfully different if people toyed with the idea.
"John," you might say, "I'm overcome with admiration for
your beautiful new toaster [wristwatch, overcoat, stereo].
I'm afraid I must ask for *tingo*."

anga-anga [noun/verb], *hakanuka-nuka* [noun], and *ngaobera* [noun] (Pascuense, Easter Island)
Nasty, useful social games.

Easter Island contains one of the most isolated cultures on
earth, both geographically and culturally. Located in the
South Pacific, 2350 miles west of the coast of Chile (which
owns it), Easter Island is home to a native culture numbering around 15,000 people today, descendants of daring
Oceanian seafarers of ages past. There had been no contact with outsiders until the 19th century. The island is
known to most people today because of the mystery of the
huge stone statues located there.

The geographical and cultural isolation have left their
marks on the language. It is as if the small-town culture of
Middle America were to be distilled to its essence. Social
psychologists talk about "enmeshed" families, in which very
close and often very volatile communications take place
between family members, as opposed to "disengaged" families in which overt communications are more cool, reserved,
and distant. Is it possible for societies to be enmeshed? Consider the social implications of a word like *anga-anga* (ON-
gah ON-gah), which, as a noun, refers to *a thought, perhaps
groundless, that one is being gossiped about, arising from one's own*

sense of guilt, and as a verb refers to *the act of thinking one is gossiped about.* My informant, who married into the culture, assures me that *anga-anga* is similar to the English word *conscience,* except it refers to something other people might know about. "It's like waiting for the other shoe to drop," my informant told me.

The term *hakanuka-nuka* (hah-kah-NOOK-ah NOOK-ah), referring to *the act of revenging oneself upon somebody for an accumulation of insults or offenses,* suggests that "forgive and forget" is not necessarily a dominant ethic. One more word, *ngaobera* (ung-OW-bear-ah), referring to *a slight inflammation of the throat produced by screaming too much,* suggests that the *hakanuka-nukas* and *angas* collide often enough to cause audible social friction.

How do words enter common usage? Simply, people use them. If there is a widespread need for a word to fit an object, action, or idea that has become important enough in a society, then a word seems to emerge. Think of these Pascuense concepts as units of meaning that have the potential to propagate and evolve as they are used by countless people over the span of many years. It doesn't take too many entry points for a word to enter a language, if the need for it is strong enough. When you know that a friend is worried that people are gossiping about him, tell him he just has a case of *anga-anga.* If a long-suffering colleague has a chance to justly revenge herself on a long-time nemesis, congratulate her on "achieving such a fine *hakanuka-nuka.*" And after somebody finishes screaming at you, calmly inform him that he is in for a bad case of *ngaobera.*

gemütlich **(German)**
Cozy, comfortable, genial, homey. [adjective]

History isn't always or entirely a matter of great men and women engaged in momentous events. Cultural changes on the level of everyday life as it is experienced by ordinary people have often proved more influential than dramatic acts like wars, revolutions, or voyages of discovery. At times, relatively short-lived cultural epochs contribute images to the wider culture, snapshots of the way one group of people actually lived at one time or another. The true origins of many of these terms are usually lost to most people who use the words a few generations later, when it has entered the language to demonstrate an abstract concept rather than the specific concrete incident that originally gave the image a name.

Such is the case with *gemütlich* (gem-OOHT-lick, with a hard "g" as in "gum"), a word that has come to mean *cozy, snug, comfortable* (when applied to a scene, usually a family scene set in a living room) and to mean (when applied to persons) *good-natured, easy-going, genial.* The dictionary definitions don't quite capture the entire image that the word is meant to evoke: Think of a middle-aged man in his housecoat, felt slippers on his feet, sitting in an overstuffed easy chair in front of a cheery fireplace. He is smoking a long pipe and reading a newspaper. He has no care in the world and is friendly to his cat and neighbors. That's *gemütlich.*

The word *gemütlich,* and the furnishings in the scene

depicted above, originated in a short-lived but vividly depicted cultural era in Germany and Austria. After the Napoleonic wars, Germany was impoverished and introspective. The cultural tendency was toward simplicity and home-based values. The period and the style of furniture are now known to historians as "Biedermeier," after Papa Biedermeier, a character featured in the early-19th-century humor magazine *Fleigende Blätter*, a worthy, bourgeois-minded fellow who apparently epitomized that popular way of life. *Gemütlichkeit* describes the overall concept of a world of *gemütlich* people in *gemütlich* settings. Don't be surprised if future cultural historians find more significance in certain editions of *Mad* magazine than the events behind a political campaign.

Zeitgeist (German)
The prevailing mood of a certain period. [noun]

When you hear somebody say that a person is "stuck in the '60s" or "has a Depression mentality," you know what is meant, even though phrases like that are vague and general, because you have a good idea of the particular *Zeitgeist* (rhymes with "right heist") that reigned in the 1960s or during the great Depression. A straightforward definition is *the spirit of the time.* The problems come in when you try to pin down exactly what that means. It isn't strictly a matter of political atmosphere, fashions, artistic trends, or mores but rather the result of a combination of all those factors. While such a measure might appear to be sociologically interesting but essentially useless (what can you do with a *Zeitgeist* except identify it?), the degree to which people are in harmony with the prevailing *Zeitgeist* can have profound effects on the way individuals live their lives and the way the business of nations is conducted.

Nobody ever plans a *Zeitgeist*, although politicians, advertising agencies, and entrepreneurs pay close attention to it, because it is a kind of summary effect of otherwise unrelated perceptions that lend a particular flavor to a time and place—perceptions that flood in upon every member of society, unbidden, triggered by different phenomena, from popular songs and catch phrases to architectural styles, political beliefs, and sexual mores. The analysis of what specifically contributes to this summing-up is best done in retrospect, so the *Zeitgeist* of a time can be fully pinned down only after the *Zeitgeist* has changed. Entrepreneurs who have a good sense of the *Zeitgeist* when it is actually occurring sometimes amass fortunes when they capture a specific commercial need at a particular moment: gourmet-cookie stores and designer clothing for toddlers, for example, were businesses that expressed and capitalized on the *Zeitgeist* of the mid-1980s.

And the ways *Zeitgeists* change can presage or even trigger profound social revolutions. Sociologist Fred Polak, in his book *The Image of the Future*, proposed that people's models of the future, which are (at least partially) a function of the *Zeitgeist*, necessarily precede large-scale societal changes. For example, before the Renaissance and the industrial revolution could have happened, people's attention had to turn away from sacred, other-worldly, spiritual matters and refocus on instrumental, earthly, pragmatic affairs. According to Polak's hypothesis, at certain pivotal points in history, it is true that "as goes the *Zeitgeist*, so goes the civilization."

fisselig (German)
Flustered to the point of incompetence. [adjective]

Have you ever been supervised so closely, nagged so incessantly, watched so intently by a critic, spouse, or boss that your performance grew sloppier as you went along? In English, you might say you were "flustered" or "jittery." In Yiddish, you would say you were "*farblonged.*" Neither of these words, however, puts any blame on the unwanted supervisorial attention that brings on this *nervousness and disintegration of composure* in the first place. The German *fisselig* (rhymes with "thistle fish") conveys a temporary state of inexactitude and sloppiness that is elicited by another person's nagging. It is the precise answer to the unkind question "What the heck is wrong with you today?"

Everyone has been in a classroom in which the teacher managed to intimidate students into speechlessness, whether or not they knew the material. Spouses trying to teach their mate how to drive an automobile often exhibit a streak of this trait. Call these not-so-helpful advisers *fisseligers*. If someone who has driven you over the edge of your ability to cope then asks you what is wrong, reply, "I'm *fisseliged.*" Your tormenter either will be stunned into puzzled silence or else will feed you your straight line by asking, "What is *that* supposed to mean?"

sitike (Apache)
In-laws who are formally committed to help during crises.
    [noun]

The English word *in-law* conveys the key defining characteristic of the ritually created nonblood relationship that
anthropologists know as "nonconsanguineal kinship": You
and your husband's brother share no genetic heritage, but
your wedding made you mutually adopted kin to one
another *in* the *law*. The cultural image of in-laws as "people
you have to put up with whether or not you like them
because they are related to your spouse" is portrayed in
America in comedy routines, jokes, situation comedies. In
other societies, where life can be tough if you don't have
help in hard times, ceremonially created kinship covenants
can be serious business.

Magic is often more than superstition. Rituals are tools
for affirming social contracts that are important to the
social group. In 1931, anthropological pioneer Bronislaw
Malinowski wrote that magic is "nothing else but an institution which fixes, organizes, and imposes upon the members
of a society the positive solution in those inevitable conflicts which arise out of human impotence in dealing with
hazardous issues by mere knowledge and technical ability."
In agricultural societies, at harvest time or in case of natural
disasters, it pays to have people who are obligated to help
you because of kinship ties. In the Apache tribe of the
Southwest, where life is demanding and often dangerous,
every pubescent girl is affirmed in a *sitike* (SIT-ee-KAY) rela-

tionship with a group of nonconsanguineal kin who are pledged to help in times of famine, illness, or disaster.

During the Apache girl's initiation ceremony, one of the most important rituals for the entire tribe, the girl and her family and clan affirm reciprocal obligations with the family and clan of her sponsor. In effect, the ceremony makes kinsmen of the tribe members who are not "blood kin," as we sometimes say in our culture. The New England poet Robert Frost said: "Home is where, when you go there, they have to take you in." An Apache might say that the *sitike* relationship consists of *people who, when you need help, have to help you.* Wouldn't that be a nice addition to the nuclear family as we know it? See *bol*, toward the end of this chapter, for a very different perspective on in-laws.

saper vivere (Italian)
To know how to handle people diplomatically. [verb]

Have you ever noticed that a blessed few people seem to have a way of getting through life without stepping on any toes? While there seem to be multitudes of people who act as if they were the only ones in the world with feelings (try a traffic jam or a crowded bus or subway to see this characteristic exhibited in full force), there is a rarer, quieter breed of person who *knows how to deal with strangers, friends, colleagues, clerks, superiors, and subordinates without bruising anybody's feelings.* The Italians would say that this person "knows how to live": *saper vivere* (suh-pear VEE-VAIR-ay). The challenge facing all of us in an increasingly hostile urban environment is not only to emulate such a person but to convince others to behave in a similarly sensitive manner. The theory of behavioral psychology is that you can increase the likelihood that a person will behave in a certain way by rewarding the person whenever he or she acts in the desired manner. The next time a rather undiplomatic person manages to get through a board meeting or a dinner party without leaving a trail of bruised egos, remark admiringly that he or she "really does *saper vivere!*"

mbuki-mvuki (Bantu)
To shuck off clothes in order to dance. [verb]

One nearly universal characteristic of human societies, no matter how different they might be in other aspects, is the social ritual known here as "having a party." Whether life is hard or easy, people seem to relish the opportunity to gather for the express purpose of not working and not acting in their normal manner. In most cultures, some form of intoxicant is used to loosen inhibitions, because a party, by definition, is the kind of ceremony in which people try to forget all the constraints and rules of everyday life, often with embarrassing results. And most cultures include some kind of dancing. When the people attending the party are single, the not-too-subtle overtones of mating ritual are added. And then, when the intoxicants have been circulating and the people have been laughing and dancing and the jukebox has been rocking, people who are ordinarily spectators in life suddenly get seized by the urge to *perform.*

It can be assumed that the Bantu-speaking people of

Africa must have a respectable heritage in the partying department, since they have a word, *mbuki-mvuki*, to describe the act of shucking off all clothing that hinders one's party performance! At least one scholar believes that this Bantu term is the direct precursor for the name that migrated up the Mississippi along with the music it described—*boogie woogie*. If you simply pronounce "boogie woogie" with a semblance of a German accent and say *mmmmmm* with relish before each word—"MMMMMbookie MMMMMvookie"—you can inform your friends about the newest/oldest term for "*I'm getting into a serious party mood.*"

suilk (Scottish)
To swallow, gulp, suck with a slobbering noise. [verb]

In some cultures, loud belching after dinner is considered the height of good manners. In other cultures, deliberate performance of digestive sounds is definitely located at the "extremely rude" end of the social spectrum. To the people of Scotland, *the act of swallowing food with an abnormal amount of noise* is considered rude enough to merit a verb of its own. When animals became sick, Scottish farmers fed them a mixture of water, meal, and salt called *suilka*-drink. To note that somebody has commenced to *suilk* (SWILLK) their soup, then, is tantamount to comparing them to a sick animal. If there are unreformed *suilkers* in your family, introduce this word as a way of making a point without drawing even more attention to the fact that one of you sounds like a hog at a trough. In cases in which you intend to draw attention to the problem-eater's auditory performance, you can use the word to enforce a lesson in manners. Don't try this on anyone who angers easily, or you might end up wearing the offender's bowl of soup.

"Where did you ever learn your extraordinary *suilking* technique?" you can ask, prompting your unsuspecting *suilker* into a perfect straight line.

"What's suilking?" the offender will undoubtedly return.

Then you can tell him about *suilk*.

rojong (Indonesian)
Mutual cooperation. [noun]

This word is closely related to another Indonesian word (*gotong*) that literally means "to carry a heavy burden together," but the Indonesians use *rojong* (roy-YONG) to connote *the relationship among a group of people who are committed to accomplish a task of mutual benefit.* In the days when America was a land of small farmers, the spirit of the barn-raising involved the kind of mutual cooperation the Indonesians refer to when they say "the villagers worked in *rojong* to build their new mosque."

Perhaps we could use a word like this in the modern world, where the need for some focused spirit of community cooperation has grown so acute that some ecologists have characterized the primary global problem as a community problem—"the tragedy of the commons." The term goes back to the days when small farmers used a "common" area in the center of town to graze their cattle or sheep. As long as no members of the community grazed more cattle than their neighbors did, everybody got along. But when the town grew large enough so that people didn't relate to one another as members of a community, first one, then many, and finally too many individuals put their own welfare above that of the group and started grazing more cattle than the land could carry. The common areas all over the country then became overgrazed and didn't do anybody any good.

Rojong may apply to people working in a variety of circumstances: community gardens, urban neighborhood tree-planting committees, block parties, PTA or church projects, cooperative day-care centers, issue-centered political action groups, energy conservation, health practices—any activities in which individuals relate to one another within a cooperative, community framework. See *tjotjog*, later in this chapter, for a related word.

lao (Chinese)
A respectful term used for older people. [adjective]

In America, most people have to make a long-distance call to talk to their grandparents. In China, the importance of the family has been a stable part of life for centuries. In the West, where the industrial revolution fragmented and scattered the traditional nuclear family, several generations no longer live together, as they still do in China. In China, grandparents are still likely to be primary caretakers of young children while their parents are working in fields, factories, or offices.

With the decline of the social role of grandparents and the rise of a youth-oriented culture, our older people are often herded into "homes," or, if they are financially healthy, into "retirement communities." And our attitudes have changed along with these demographics. The older worker is no longer respected as a source of wisdom by the newer members of a work force, who are interested in learning new methods, and older members of the family are no longer universally revered as a link with the way things always have been done. Now that it looks like the demography is changing again, it is likely that our attitudes will change as well. With new attitudes comes the need for new words.

The coming demographic change can be foreseen in the statistics that indicate a shift in the median age of our population: As the baby-boom generation grows older, our attitudes toward older people are bound to change. In the event that that change indicates a turn to more respectful modes of address, perhaps we should adopt the Chinese honorific *lao* (rhymes with "cow"), which can apply equally to one's great-grandfather or the senior member of an assembly line or management team. When social prejudices change, members of oppressed groups usually take the initiative in changing the language by insisting on respectful terms of address; the insistence by nonwhite males on being addressed as "Mister" was a linguistic component of the civil rights revolution; the advent of "Ms." as a nonsexist means of address went along with the women's movement. Perhaps the "gray rights" movement of the 1990s will be marked by your grandpa Tom's insistence on being addressed as "*Lao* Grandpa Tom."

kyoikumama (Japanese)
**Mother who pushes her children into academic achieve-
ment.** [noun]

Education is serious business for young folks in Japan,
because performance in primary school determines whether
or not a student will get into one of the better middle
schools, and a middle school performance leads either to
one of the best senior highs or to a less prestigious high
school. And the best high schools are the ones that train
their students to pass the grueling entrance examinations
for the best universities. If a student is not admitted to a
prestigious university, that student's life and career are, in
some sense, "ruined," for the caliber of one's university
determines the caliber of the job one gets after college. And
since the firm one joins after college is often one's employer
for life, this is serious indeed. The pressure on Japanese
students is intense, and it begins at home. In the most
extreme, and not terribly rare, instances, the young person's life is directed toward academic achievement by the
kind of mother who is bitterly referred to as a *kyoikumama*
(KYOH-ee-koo-mama). It is not a complimentary term.

From toddlerhood, the *kyoikumama* (literally, "education
mama") aims her child's life at the college entrance exams,
with exhortations, special treats for achievement, pressure,
and special tutoring. This word is particularly well suited for
contemporary America, for a significant percentage of the
upscale child-bearing population is already entrenched in
this way of thinking: Some parents attempt to preregister

children for prestigious private schools even before the children are born, and the notion that children can be crammed with facts via flash cards and drills even before they can walk has found a following. In America, however, the phenomenon is not confined to mothers, so it might be more proper to refer to *kyoikuparents* the next time you see a pregnant woman playing Bach to her fetus by means of earphones on her abdomen, or a father barraging his bewildered one-year-old with algebraic equations on flash cards.

carità pelosa (Italian)
Generosity with an ulterior motive. [noun]

The casinos of Reno and Las Vegas offer special junkets for high rollers and low rollers alike: The high rollers are picked up by private plane and are treated to lavish accommodations, free of charge; the low rollers are offered low bus fares and free chips that are often worth *more* than the price of the bus trip. How generous! Lobbyists for political causes are also generous folks, taking members of Congress out for expensive lunches, offering them the use of exclusive hunting lodges and other blandishments. How thoughtful! Perhaps you know someone who is especially generous to people who might help in business, social life, or political endeavors. The Italians, who cast a jaundiced eye on such largess, call it *carità pelosa*—literally, "hairy generosity." In some countries, cultures, societies, and neighborhoods, outright bribery is frowned upon, but *generosity with an obvious ulterior motive* is considered good manners: Bottles of liquor for the health inspector if you run a restaurant, for example.

Next time somebody is especially generous and you suspect an ulterior motive, look more closely at the "gift" and see if the generosity is "hairy."

confianza (Spanish)
Unshakable, firm belief in someone. [noun]

Linguistically, *confianza* (kon-fee-ON-zuh) is related to the English word *confidence*, but there is a world of difference. To have confidence in someone is to demonstrate a modicum of faith, perhaps even a great deal of faith. But it doesn't imply, as *confianza* does, a combination of utterly eternal, unshakable reliance, trust, confidence, and unconditional social support that *confianza* does. Similarly, you can ask somebody to keep some private matter "in confidence," but if you were to ask a Spanish-speaking person to speak *en confianza*, you would be asking, in effect, to commit to your trust his innermost soul secrets. In essence, *confianza* is confidence that differs from the English version quantitatively to such a degree that there is a qualitative difference. *Confianza* goes down to the spiritual marrow.

In Spain, *confianza* went along with long-term friendships and especially solid family relationships. We need to introduce this term into our society, because this sort of trust doesn't come about automatically in an era where your best friend might be someone you've known for only a few years. If you want to demonstrate utter, uncondi-

tional support for someone, say that you have *confianza.*
Then, when you are asked what that means, you have the
opportunity to point out that your social support is deeper
than you can convey with any word in the English language.
Tell them that unconditional love is to love as *confianza* is
to trust.

épater les bourgeois (French)
To deliberately shock people who have conventional values.
    [verb]

What do you say when your teenage daughter shows up with
her head shaved and a large pink tattoo of a rat etched into
her pate? If you exhibit shock at this sight, you will undoubtedly be fulfilling all her expectations. Similarly, how do you
evaluate the aesthetic value of your son's newest record,
which he plays at highest volume and which was apparently
recorded in a slaughterhouse? In both cases, you are experiencing an age-old phenomenon that is so common,
finding new forms from generation to generation, that the
French have a phrase for it, *épater les bourgeois* (eh-pah-TAY
lay boor-JWAH), which literally means *to amaze the middle
class.* It is one of the oldest social games in the book.

In order to qualify for this category, the candidate's
behavior must be more than merely raucous. The annual
antics of college kids in Fort Lauderdale might qualify as a
rite of spring, for instance, but the punk rocker's devotion
to truly creative ways of shocking normal sensibilities is
much closer to the spirit of the phrase. If such behavior

weren't shocking, *épater les bourgeois* wouldn't be so fashionable, particularly among rebellious adolescents. So if you want to shock the shockers, just take another tip from the French and act *blasé.*

tjotjog (Javanese)
Harmonious congruence in human affairs. [verb]

In America, a melting pot of many traditions, we have many different ideas of social harmony. "May the best man win," "Don't rock the boat" and "Look out for number one" are common testaments to our collective ethos. In Java, a far less heterogeneous and competitive society than our own, where religion, occupation, morality, and family life mesh, it is possible for a different attitude toward social harmony to emerge. The concept of *tjotjog* (CHOT-chog) epitomizes this. While it might not be practicable in our society, it does furnish food for thought, as well as hope that at least somewhere in the world people have achieved a resonance between cosmic harmony, intellectual and aesthetic correctness, and cooperative family relationships. In *The Interpretation of Cultures*, Clifford Geertz, an anthropologist who studied the Javanese culture, had this to say about it:

> *Tjotjog* means to fit, as a key does in a lock, as an efficacious medicine does to a disease, as a solution does to an arithmetic problem, as a man does with a woman he marries.... If your opinion agrees with mine, we *tjotjog*; if the meaning of my name fits my character (and if it brings me luck), it is said to be *tjotjog*. Tasty food, correct theories, good manners, comfortable surroundings, gratifying outcomes are all *tjotjog*. In the broadest and most

abstract sense, two items *tjotjog* when their coincidence forms a coherent pattern which gives to each a significance and a value it does not in itself have.... *Tjotjog* is a peculiarly Javanese idea, but the notion that life takes on its true import when human actions are tuned to cosmic conditions is widespread.

Tjotjog is not unknown in our society, but people certainly yearn for more of it than we seem to encounter in daily life. Only rarely in our work or play do *cooperative efforts mesh together to an almost supernatural degree, through a combination of practice, skill, confidence, mutual regard, and timing.* But we know it when we see it. Everybody recognizes the high degree of *tjotjog* involved when a basketball player passes the ball behind his back without even looking to see if somebody is there, because he knows his teammate will *tjotjog*. In televised sports, which might be likened to an ecumenical folk religion in this society, a passer and receiver who have just executed a particularly harmonious play in a football game often engage in elaborate hand-shaking and exchange of (often vulgar) slang expressions celebrating their success, precisely because they recognize they achieved a state that could be described as *tjotjog*. In business, people tend to imitate these expressions. Perhaps *tjotjog* ought to be introduced into the world of sports as the latest alternative to the "high five," which would guarantee that this new verbal custom thence would be broadcast with great rapidity, by sportscasters, on Sunday afternoons all across the country. (See *rojong*, earlier in this chapter, for a related word.)

tartle (**Scottish**)
To hesitate in recognizing a person or thing. [verb]

We all have found ourselves, at least once, in the embarrassing position of talking to somebody who has been introduced before but whose name temporarily escapes all attempts at recall. If you recover quickly enough to avoid terminal embarrassment and remember the name of the fellow partygoer or business acquaintance, you have committed an act common enough for the Scottish people to have coined a word for it: They would say that you *tartled* (TAR-tul). In fact, if you want to distract attention from your moment of hesitation and perhaps steer the conversation toward untranslatable words (and away from your social gaffe), just say: "Sorry about my temporary *tartle*!" Of course, you can always use the word as a bit of a gleeful prod when somebody does it to you: "Don't worry about it, old boy—we all *tartle* at one time or another!"

dozywocie (**Polish**)
**Parental contract with children guaranteeing lifelong
    support. [noun]**

By the end of the 20th century, America will be a predominantly aging population, and the problems of caring for the elderly, which are already beginning to cause family and social problems, will be highly visible. We might think of adopting a custom from the Polish people, who make a retirement contract with their children. *Dozywocie* (doszh-VOCH), which means "support for life," involves a distribution of property at retirement (rather than a will that distributes property at death). The parents make an arrangement with the son or daughter in whom they have the greatest amount of confidence and then bequeath *an additional share of property in exchange for a promise that the offspring thus honored will support the aging parents for life.*

The problem with this custom, which is backed up not only by a legal contract but by strong social pressure and ostracism against those who break it, is that it turns retirees into dependents, which is not often a desirable situation. In Poland, where the cynical viewpoint is that children often treat their parents exceptionally well as they approach retirement age, but don't often continue this lavish treatment after the contract has been notarized and their bequest received, the popular saying is, "You ride to the notary on feathers, but you trudge back home on foot."

nakhes (Yiddish)
A mixture of pleasure and pride, particularly the kind that a parent receives from a child. [noun]

When your young daughter spends all morning cutting and pasting and drawing and then proudly presents you with a valentine, the feeling that wells up inside is the emotion that Jews describe as *nakhes* (NOKH-ess, with the KH pronounced in the Hebrew manner, in the back of the throat). It is a special kind of pleasure, a feeling of love infused with sensations of pride and joy. It is something one *receives,* as in:

"May you get only *nakhes* from your son!" A secondary and far less emotionally powerful meaning is a general feeling of gratification one receives from creating something that turns out well: "I get a lot of *nakhes* from working in my garden, especially at harvest time" or "I got *nakhes* from building that chair."

tsuris (Yiddish)
Grief and trouble, especially the kind that only a son or daughter can give you. [noun]

You might say that *tsuris* (TSOO-rihss) is the opposite of *nakhes*: It means a feeling of being overwhelmed by bad news, of extraordinary aggravation, a sensation of seeing something or someone turn against you. A daughter who achieves her phi beta kappa gives you *nakhes*, but a son who ends up in San Quentin is a source of *tsuris*.

All cases of *tsuris* are not as extreme as a felony conviction by a beloved offspring. Growing up seems to offer a mixture of *nakhes*, and *tsuris*, and the degree of *nakhes* one gets from seeing a successful and happy offspring is often measured against the amount of *tsuris* one had to suffer along the way. In *The Joys of Yiddish*, Leo Rosten puts it this way:

"And how many children do you have?"
"None."
"So what do you do for *tsuris*?"

These are extremely useful words. When a child is born, it is appropriate to say, "May she only bring you *nakhes*." And when someone shows you a photograph of his son, with obvious pride, you can say: "He must give you much *nakhes.*" Conversely, when somebody tells you about his gall bladder operation or a recent IRS audit, it is appropriate to say, "Oy, such *tsuris*!"

bol (Mayan)
Stupid in-laws. [noun/adjective]

The Apaches have the *sitike* relationship, which is a very positive kind of in-law-ship. In Poland, there is a similar kind of kinship obligation, which can be regarded in a more grudging kind of way, in regard to relations who are considered *swojak.* But the Mayans of southern Mexico and Honduras use the same word—*bol* (BOWL)—to serve for in-laws as well as stupidity! Variations of this root word also indicate the kind of dazed befuddlement that accompanies a blow on the head, or the kind of stupor that can be induced by drugs.

In many traditions, indirect speech is used to insult people without their knowledge (see *sanza* in chapter three). If you have a lot of trouble dealing with your in-laws' lack of sensitivity or manners or intelligence, why don't you just suggest "Mayan bowling" every time they ask what you want to do? Then, while they look at you with puzzled expressions, laugh like a hyena.

ramé (**Balinese**)
Crowded, bustling, chaotic, hectic social environment.
   [noun/adjective]

Social scientists talk about different cultures and families as being either "enmeshed," meaning that everybody is closely concerned with one another's business and very highly dependent upon one another, or "disengaged," meaning that everybody is independent, autonomous, and doesn't mind the others' business. In our North American culture, with its strong strain of individualism, is a disengaged culture. Balinese culture, however, is considered to be one of the most highly enmeshed cultures in the world. What this means is that people on the island of Bali always seem to do things in groups, even the most elementary tasks. A political meeting, a dramatic group (puppetry and other dramas are important parts of Balinese social life), even a collection of people who decide to fetch some fruit or firewood always seem to involve many more people than technically necessary. And they all seem to chatter away about the most intimate details of one another's lives.

When a social group tends to include many people in activities, and when those people are inordinately involved with and concerned about one another's lives, *the social atmosphere tends to look chaotic, bustling, hectic, and crowded* to Western eyes. To the Balinese, this is one of their primary social values, which they call *ramé* (RAH-may). And they have a sense of humor about their hivelike approach to life, using the words *bebek-bebekan* (literally, "ducklike") to describe the way groups of Balinese tend to quack and waddle along together, as if in formation.

In America, a melting pot of many cultures, people from WASP families, where dinnertime is sedate, individuals are autonomous, and conversation is polite and tends toward the impersonal, sometimes go into culture shock when they dine at an Italian or a Jewish home, where individuals are interdependent, conversation is lively and even argumentative, and people seem to poke into one another's private affairs a great deal. If you are from an enmeshed family and a friend or spouse whose background is more disengaged shows signs of shock at exposure to your chaotic social atmosphere, just smile pleasantly and tell them about *ramé*, a value from a culture where this brand of chaos is even more intense.

CHAPTER TWO

You Are What You Say

Words of Power

The words of a living language are like creatures: they are alive. Each word has a physical character, a look and a personality, an ancestry, an expectation of life and death, a hope of posterity. Some words strike us as beautiful, some ugly, some evil. The word *glory* seems to shine; the common word for excrement seems to smell. There are holy words, like the proper name of God, pronounced only once a year in the innermost court of Jerusalem's Temple. There are magic words, spells to open gates and safes, summon spirits, put an end to the world. What are magic spells but magic spellings? Words sing to us, frighten us, impel us to self-immolation and murder. They belong to us; they couple at our order, to make what have well been called the aureate words of poets and the inkhorn words of pedants. We can keep our words alive, or at our caprice we can kill them—though some escape and prosper in our despite.

Morris Bishop, *Good Usage, Bad Usage, and Usage*

*W*e create the world every day when we utter words. Yet we are rarely aware of this awesome act. The power of words is woven so tightly into our daily lives that we hardly ever take time to marvel at it. Our ancestors knew, though: It is no accident that many of the world's religious scriptures assert that the universe was created by a word. As far as human evolution goes, the invention of language was the one event that hurtled our primate ancestors beyond the slow, random process of natural selection. The evolution of life on this planet leaped into overdrive as soon as *Homo sapiens* started using brains, lips, tongues, and vocal cords to transmit information.

When we started exchanging memes (units of meaning), our progress toward ever-increasing consciousness no longer depended on the exchange of genes. Because of words and the ways we have learned to use them, biological evolution is no longer the means by which our species changes and grows. The evolution of language, however, is continuing. To the degree that languages can change as an effect of improved communication technologies, the evolution of language is *accelerating*. Perhaps the most miraculous aspect of linguistic evolution is the way languages grow and change because of and in response to the uses ordinary people find for them, not because a group of specialists engineered or planned it. It is entirely possible that by reading this book you are participating in a significant linguistic revolution.

The first magicians and the first technologists were the same people—the ones who used coded shouts to organize hunts, to convey knowledge, to construct abstractions. Word magic was the original magic, for the naming of things and processes is the first step in gaining power over them. The science of words is relatively young, but the magic of words is much older. As language evolved in thousands of different linguistic communities around the world, many different cultures developed special words to describe and

enhance the power of words. Words about words are not
limited to philologists in universities. As we shall see in this
chapter, those preindustrial societies that are often mistak-
enly described as "primitive" often possess highly sophisticated terminology for metalinguistic practices—words that
have meanings on more than one level.

Indirect speech, for example, seems to be a universal
phenomenon. People in every culture seem to have a fond-
ness for communicating via circumlocutions, metaphors,
analogies, similes—everything but coming right out and saying directly what is on their minds. Here, we might dismiss
this practice as "beating around the bush." In other cultures, however, one must often be very careful in order to
avoid getting to the point: Among the Kiriwina tribespeople
of the Trobriand Islands, for example, you cannot utter
mokita without fear of serious social disruption, so you have
to use *biqa viseki* to refer indirectly to unspeakable truths.
Sometimes, intolerable social pressures must be vented verbally in a safe way, without fear of setting off a riot, war, or
a family disturbance: In New Guinea, you can hurl *sanzas* at
people without their knowledge, and in China, when you
can't cuss out anybody in your vicinity because they all out-
rank you, it is possible to resort to *majie.*

The jungles of New Guinea are not the only place where
words are used as weapons. Cocktail parties and classrooms,
scientific conferences and book reviews, PTA meetings and
playgrounds are all arenas for various verbal skirmishes. It is
crucially important that verbal warriors know the difference
between the Italian phrase *far secco qualcuno,* the German *Trep-*

penwitz and the French *esprit de l'escalier* if they hope to survive a cocktail party where the social vectors are fast and furious.

Several cultures have specific words for words of power and magic. The Sanskrit word *mantra* literally means "mind tool," and in Indonesia, a specific phrase, *holopis kuntul baris,* is believed to have a definite physical effect on the person who utters it. And the Huron word *orenda* is a must for all word magicians, for it offers a clue to the connection between willpower and word power.

We are all magicians. We are all shamans. Our power over ourselves, our world, our fellow word magicians, often depends on how we use words. The more we know about words and the way words are used to confront or to avoid conflict, the more options we have in our lives. There is fun to be found in the pages that follow, but there is also power.

mokita (Kiriwina, New Guinea)
Truth everybody knows but nobody speaks. [noun]

In every culture and in many different kinds of social encounters, from back-fence gossip to high-level negotiations, the words that are *not* voiced can be more important than the ones that are spoken aloud. People who share the same language, nationality, kinship, clanship, or other cultural heritage have special agreements about the meanings of words and symbols; they also have agreements about the meanings of unspoken words and other symbols that are hidden or alluded to but never directly displayed. Within a family, the alcoholism of a relative is an ever-present unspoken truth, just as the subject of AIDS is an inevitable unspoken truth in a singles bar. Unwritten laws of many games, from the playground to the battlefield, govern the conduct of formal encounters. And in every speech act there is a dichotomy in the mind of each participant between public utterances and private thoughts. At times, most of what we say is what we don't say.

The old folk-story about the emperor's new clothes reveals that we in the West have long acknowledged the power of unspoken truths. But in English we don't have a specific word to refer to unspoken truths. The Kiriwina tribespeople of the Trobriand Islands, however, use the word *mokita* (moe-KEE-tah) to refer to *the unspoken truths of certain social situations that everybody knows but nobody talks about—directly.* This distinction is a social convention, but it is such a strong social convention that it literally alters the perceptions of the individuals within that society. Of course, sly allusions and other forms of disguised speech can refer to those unspeakable facts that everybody in a tightly knit community tends to know—who cheated whom, who is sleeping with whom, who is out to get whom, and the specific historical instances associated with each act. The use of indirect speech (see *biqa viseki* in this chapter) is raised to a high art in cultures like that of the Kiriwina, where direct speech about taboo topics can lead to violent death (see *biga peula* in this chapter).

There are times when *mokita* helps shield people from truths they would rather not face, and there are times when it is simply an act of kindness to recognize it. If your brother or friend has a very slow child or one that closely resembles his best friend, the whole subject is better left *mokita.* When people in our culture want to "get down to business" or to "stop beating around the bush," they often say, "But the bottom line is . . ." A heftier version of "bottom line," one that refers directly to a situation that everybody knows about but nobody talks about (who cheated whom, who is sleeping with whom, and so on), would be, "Let's get down to the *mokita.*" The potency of this phrase, if accepted into the language, would make a qualitative difference as well as provide an increased emphasis: Speaking about *mokita* can mean that you are obligated to *do* something about it.

biga peula (Kiriwina, New Guinea)
Potentially disruptive, unredeemable true statements.
[noun]

In most cultures around the world, certain words or phrases are almost never used because they invariably lead to physical violence, and often to the death of either the person who utters them or the person to whom the words were directed. In the West, these are known as "fighting words," and both their nature and their effect seem to vary from culture to culture. In some cultures and circumstances, insults are considered friendly. And in some countries, an insult to one's horse or manner of dress can be far more odious than the worst kinship-related insults.

The Kiriwina tribespeople of the Trobriand Islands vest great power in certain unspoken truths (see *mokita* in this chapter). There are many things in Kiriwina life that everybody is presumed to know about but that nobody talks about directly. The Kiriwina use the phrase *biga peula* (literally, "hard words," pronounced BEE-kuh POOL-uh) to refer to *direct references to certain unspoken truths.* Social contracts among the Kiriwina, like social contracts among any other group of people, consist of many arrangements, spoken and unspoken, by which the members of the society agree to pay attention to certain things or to *ignore* certain things, in order to promote the smooth functioning of the society. Among the Kiriwina, so much power resides in the unspoken social contracts that the rare use of the *biga peula* can reorder the reality of individuals and entire social groups by forcing them to pay attention to that which is commonly ignored. So much power is vested in these words that the act of "speaking hard words" is irrevocable. Even the most vicious insults can be atoned for by the right kind of apologies and/or reparations. But a Kiriwina cannot redeem "hard words" by apologizing.

This phenomenon is not confined to the Kiriwina. In many companies, you can get yourself fired by saying out loud what everybody knows to be true: "The boss is an idiot." In every marriage, there are phrases that partners never use, no matter how bitter the argument, unless they are ready for the marriage to end: "I've had a mistress for six years" is *biga peula* for a husband to say to a wife, just as "You aren't Tommy's father" is a *biga peula* for a wife to say to a husband. A useful phrase in many of these situations might be: "Wait! Don't say what you are about to say. It could be *biga peula* for us." But in the rough-and-tumble world of business and other pragmatic enterprises like war and marriage, it is sometimes necessary to speak openly of that which is normally left unspoken. When a board of directors, a platoon, or a family approaches certain critical decisions, it is time for somebody to take the chance of suffering extreme social consequences for the sake of a possible breakthrough by deliberately speaking *biga peula*.

Among the Kiriwina, there are only a few alternatives to combat once *biga peula* have been spoken. One of these alternatives is a ritual that averts outright violence; however, one anthropologist reported that this ritual produced more fear and anxiety than any other public event he had witnessed. See the definition of *biritilulo* in chapter five for more details of the terror-producing yam-comparing ceremony of the Kiriwina.

biqa viseki (Kiriwina, New Guinea)
Use of metaphors as disguised speech. [noun]

Because there are many instances in which the "hard truth" cannot be voiced directly, the Kiriwina tribespeople have developed elaborate forms of indirect speech. *The ability of linguistic tokens to point to a multiplicity of meanings* is one of the great strengths and mysteries of human language. In English, literary devices such as metaphor, analogy, and simile are used in poetry and prose to create levels within levels of meaning. Among the Kiriwina, the use of indirect speech is an art and science, and metaphors, analogies, simile, and double entendres are called *biqa viseki* (BEE-kuh viz-

EHK-ee). In English, these figures of speech are generally used only for clichés or euphemisms, and more complex forms of multiple meaning are left to writers and comedians. Among the Kiriwina, *biqa viseki* is part of the vernacular and is used in the context of an extemporaneous performance rather than a premeditated formal document.

The old story of the birds and the bees is one variety of *biqa viseki* that we are familiar with in our society: Many American parents are too shy about sexual matters to discuss them frankly with their children, so flustered fathers and shame-faced mothers describe the adventures of the birds and the bees and hope their offspring can put the analogy into the proper anatomical perspective. While sexual matters are the cause for much clever use of tropes (particularly by Shakespeare, who saw fit to embed bawdy puns, metaphors, and similes in some of the greatest works of English literature), sex is not the only subject of indirect speech.

What advantages do veiled allusions, multiple meanings, symbolic resonances have over plain, ordinary, direct speech? For one thing, metaphors create a degree of richness of interpretation that opens the listener to a much wider range of association than ordinary speech does. And the common use of metaphors can form the basis of a kind of metalanguage, a way to offer commentary on the deeper meaning of one's words. Political buzzwords such as "law and order," for example, can evoke a whole constellation of issues concerning social values. In complex matters of human emotion, where subtleties and contradictions abound, the proper use of metaphor, analogy, and simile can provide the listener with embedded advice about how to think about the matter under discussion: "I'm trying to tell you that I love you," for example, is often said indirectly.

The use of "veiled references" can serve to protect people from conflict, embarrassment, and other secondary social consequences of truth-telling. They can also be used to convey multiple levels of meaning to different people in the same audience, so that friends or initiates will understand the hidden allusions in the words, whereas strangers or the uninitiated will miss them. Because *biqa viseki* demands increased attention, thought, and evaluation on the part of listeners, it can be an effective tool for persuasion. Among the Kiriwina, cleverness in the use of *biqa viseki* is actually a form of word magic, as anthropologist Annette Weiner points out: "Words...are the formal elements that create the potential power to enable speech to shift or recreate perceived realities."

Most people have the power to "shift the reality" of their social groups; most of the time we choose not to. In daily life, you can cause quite a stir among your friends and acquaintances by paying attention to those instances when the use of euphemism reaches absurd proportions: "Wait a minute," you can cry. "Isn't it time to cut the *biqa viseki*?"

sanza (Zande, New Guinea)
Disguised insult. [noun]

All societies demand a certain degree of politeness in speech and action in order to preserve public order. In some societies, the use of invective against strangers is considered to be borderline acceptable public behavior (think of a Roman traffic jam or a heated discussion on a Manhattan sidewalk). In other societies, direct display of hostility can lead to serious trouble. This is where nasty forms of indirect speech like *sanza* (SON-zah, rhymes with "Honda") comes in handy. Among the Azande, people who have a particular grudge against someone else will use *sanza, a circumlocutory form of speech that employs words and gestures to create hidden malicious meanings to apparently polite, innocuous speech.* A weak Western equivalent might be the sly wink seen only by a sympathetic colleague and hidden from the person to whom it is directed, in conjunction with an ironic reference such as "I really like your enthusiastic little poodle, Mrs. Johnson," or "It's been a real pleasure working with you, Tom," or "Well, isn't that *special?*"

The art of *sanza* lies in the cleverness that must be used to provide a plausible alibi for every hidden meaning and secret gesture, should the butt of the maliciousness begin to catch on. This form of disguised speech is prevalent among slaves and servants. If a butler, in the presence of other servants, were to slightly elevate one eyebrow and say to his master, who has been putting on weight: "You are certainly becoming quite a man, sir," he would be practicing a dangerous form of servant *sanza.* Similarly, to be caught insulting someone is serious business among the Zande, so it is very important that the user of *sanza* have an alibi: "Oh, I was really talking about your lawn, not your face...." And the Zande don't confine their secret gestures to winks or slightly raised eyebrows. Another part of the art is to use a gesture that is common enough so that it doesn't arouse suspicion on the part of the target, but distinctive enough so that it tips off your cohorts to the presence of secondary meanings to your words.

To the censored, the oppressed, the downtrodden, and those who are merely terrified of rocking the boat, the idea of covert defiance might sound very appealing. If you and your coworkers are not allowed to air your grievances against a martinet of a boss, you probably use a primitive form of *sanza* to show defiance. Why not try to slip a few secret gestures into your conversation? "Yes sir, Mr. Johnson, I'll get to that [twitch, twitch], *right away.*"

majie (Chinese)
To curse the street. [verb]

Cursing, swearing, muttering oaths, and hurling expletives seem a universal form of human linguistic behavior, but the degree of propriety assigned to such outbursts appears to be highly culture-bound. Acceptable behavior in one venue might be a capital offense in another. The place of such activities in a society or even a particular neighborhood seems to be a function of community values and standards: It matters very much, from place to place and time to time, whether the particular words used in this emotion-venting ritual are theologically, scatologically, or sexually related. In some places, you can say anything you want about your neighbor's place of worship or lack of hygiene, but if you mention his mother or sister, you'd better be prepared for serious trouble. In other cultures, the key determinant is not the content of the utterances, but their *target*—it matters little what you say, as long as you don't say it to the wrong person.

In China, where family ties and Confucian social customs have long bound individual behavior into the confines of well-understood and relatively polite roles, it is considered the height of indiscretion to directly hurl imprecations at many of the people who might be the most likely targets of great personal anger. Men and elders have especially privileged positions. *Majie* (MAH-jyeh), literally "to curse or revile the street," however, is acceptable.

Can't tell off your in-law, your husband, your father? Run out and tell it to the road. In China, people, especially women, are not considered crazy if they are found talking to the street in strongly pejorative terms. Perhaps we ought to institute the practice of *majie* in Western cultures and redirect the hostility that is often aimed at drivers or pedestrians to where it truly belongs—the doggone blankety-blank road! Or if a very large, unpleasant-looking person cuts in front of you in a market, wouldn't it be great if custom allowed you to wait until he leaves the market to start voicing loud opinions? And when people look around for the target of your invective, you can defuse any potential hostility by shrugging your shoulders, pointing down at the floor, and saying *majie*!

For those who believe that venting hostile impulses rather than keeping them bottled up is the healthiest way to deal with life's frustrations, you can do your stressed-out friend a favor by telling him or her to go out and spout *majie* for a while—and then demonstrate how it's done. When your husband or wife breaks dishes, accompanied by various imprecations, appreciate the fact that he or she isn't talking to you ... directly. It's *majie.* If you are a parent, you can use this word to label the behavior of a teenage daughter who, a few minutes after you've grounded her for the weekend, throws her hair dryer across the room because it isn't working properly. Tell your spouse that your offspring telling off inanimate objects is "just *majie.*"

esprit de l'escalier (French) and *Treppenwitz* (German)
Clever remark that comes to mind when it is too late to utter it. [nouns]

The French said it first when they came up with a name for that special kind of unspoken word or phrase, *the clever rejoinder to the public insult, or the brilliantly witty remark that comes into your mind only after you have left the party: Esprit de l'escalier* (ehs-PREE duh les-kall-YAY) literally means "the spirit of the staircase." Sometimes, this feeling about what you ought to have said at a crucial moment can haunt you for the rest of your life.

If it happens to you or a friend, and if you are feeling Continental, the French idiom is probably appropriate. In other cases, however, the German derivative *Treppenwitz* (TRAP-pen-vitz, rhymes with "Jack and Fritz") may prevail, since it carries the concept further, to historical dimensions.

In addition to referring to the kind of remark that occurs to a person when it is too late, it also applies to events that appear to be the result of a joke played by fate or history. The Battle of New Orleans in the War of 1812 is a classic example. Andrew Jackson led his irregulars to the war's greatest victory for the Americans, but because of the slow communications of the era, it was fought two weeks after the British and Americans had signed a peace treaty!

far secco qualcuno (Italian)
To render someone speechless with a cutting comment.
[verb]

For those occasions when you or somebody else is quick enough to think of a devastating comeback before reaching the staircase (see *esprit de l'escalier* earlier in this chapter), the Italians have a phrase that translates "to leave someone dry": *far secco qualcuno* (far SECK-oh kwall-KOOH-noh). The literal image is of a person who can't speak because all his saliva has dried up. When you relate an outrageously shocking statement that somebody made to you and you are asked how you replied, it is perfectly acceptable to say, "I couldn't say anything! I was *fatto secco* at the idiocy of the remark."

An infamous instance of a public figure who rendered another public figure *far secco qualcuno* before a national audience is attributed to rock musician Frank Zappa. On a television talk show, the host, known for his aggressive obnoxiousness, asked Zappa: "Does that long hair make you a girl?" Zappa, remarking on a well-known physical characteristic of the nasty host, replied: "Does your wooden leg make you a table?"

Since we are proposing that this phrase should be adopted for English usage, it is better to forget about the full proper conjugation; simply mutter, "That left her *secco* didn't it?" when you witness *a perfect rejoinder that leaves the deserving target speechless.*

orenda (Huron)
The power of voiced, focused will—the opposite of *kismet* or fate. [noun]

When the Huron Indians of the northeastern United States use the word *orenda* (oar-END-uh), which literally means "song," they really are conjuring the concept of mystic influence of incantation, *the kind of power that mortals can summon to combat the blind forces of fate.* The English *prayer* doesn't convey its pride, and *spell* is too sinister. Among the Huron, one meaning of *orenda* is conveyed by the image of the cicada, composing its early morning song in order to make sure the day will be hot and the corn will ripen properly. The idea that the Huron were trying to convey something more universal than simple animism was noted by anthropologist R. R. Marett, who interprets the true nature of the word as "a bittersweet blend of fear and hope—of humility and confidence. Thus, on the one hand 'he is arrayed in his *orenda*' means that one is trying to obtain one's desire, and hence is equivalent to saying 'he hopes or expects.' On the other hand, however, 'he lays down his own *orenda*' stands for 'he prays,' indicating submission in the face of a superior power."

The use of a word that can mean hope, power, focused intention, and prayer to a higher power, without conveying either a sense of helpless passivity in the face of a coldly deterministic fate or the overweening pride the Greeks call *hubris*, has a place in the modern Western world, as a counterspell to negative affirmations like "I guess it was *kismet*," or "Whatever will be will be." Just counter with: "I'm arrayed in my *orenda* regarding the Johnson contract," or "I'm deeply concerned about the way our relationship is going, so I'm going to lay down my own *orenda* on it."

attaccabottoni (Italian)
A doleful bore who buttonholes people and tells sad, pointless tales. [noun]

Words have the power to hypnotize if they are wielded by a skilled hypnotist. Words have the power to enthrall when they are spoken by a charismatic personality. And words have the power to put the most lively person to sleep when they fall into the hands of that most dreaded conversational specialist, the bore. Volumes could be written about the many varieties of bore to be found in small towns in Indiana, villages in the New Guinea Highlands, or cocktail parties in Manhattan. Of the several differing schools of bore theory, all the competing factions agree that the worst of all is *the doleful bore, the kind who buttonholes hapless acquaintances or total strangers* who are too kind or innocent to flee at the first word, and proceeds to tell long and pointless stories of misfortune, unhappiness, and bad circumstances. The Italians have a word for this type. If you are trying to warn somebody to avoid even slight signs of recognition, including eye contact, tell your friend to "watch out for the *attaccabottoni*" (rhymes with "a lot of baloney").

The word literally means "buttonholer" and can be used as a verb. When referring to the unusually aggressive bore who succeeded in detaining you on the telephone on your way out the door, you can say you were *attaccabotoed*.

sbottonarsi (Italian)
To open up, reveal one's opinion or feelings. [verb]

While *attaccabottoni* are generally people who ought to keep their mouths shut, others may err too far in the opposite direction, keeping so much to themselves that you wish they would come out and speak their mind. *Sbottonarsi* (sbot-uh-NARE-see) means literally "to unbutton oneself," and this is precisely what you want the close-mouthed individual to do: to open up, to let something escape through that wall of reserve. It can be used as a way of catching the attention of these problem people, who are sometimes unaware of how disconcerting their aloofness might be: "Come on," you might say, "why don't you just *sbottonarsi*?"

holopis kuntul baris (**Indonesian**)
A phrase uttered in order to gain extra strength when
carrying heavy objects. [noun]

If this phrase works for you as well as the Indonesians claim
it works for them, it is a rare, valuable example of a practical
magic spell: *an utterance that can ease an onerous physical task*
by conjuring hidden reserves of strength. Everybody grunts when
lifting objects, due to the contraction of the solar plexus,
and martial arts experts utter a sharp cry when they strike
a blow in order to focus musculoskeletal energy, so there
must be *some* physiological reason why uttering a phrase
might impart extra strength for toting a barge or lifting a
bale. The magical part is choosing the right phrase. In the
age of the tall ships, when navigational lingo influenced
the language the way automobile-related jargon now influ-
ences contemporary colloquial English, the phrase *heave,*
heave, heave, HO was used by groups of people doing muscular work in unison.

Unlike most of the other words in this book, which are
directed at the acts of communication between people,
holopis kuntul baris (hoh-LOPE-iss COON-tool BAH-riss) is
meant for solitary use, when you are trying to summon the
strength to move a desk or lift a television set. The use of
the voice to focus physical energy in combat manifests in
the battle cries of warriors around the world, and in a pure
form in the *ki-ai*, or "soul cry," that accompanies karate
blows. Football players shout in unison when they leave the
huddle. But *holopis kuntul baris* does not have to be limited

to muscular strength. In an extended sense, it can be regarded as one instance out of a whole secret vocabulary of energy-summoning words—symbolic reminders of every person's ability to tap hidden reserves of strength. You can even make up your own *holopis kuntul baris* for other situations—physical, intellectual, social—where peak performance is required. In the famous children's story, the Little Engine That Could repeated to itself, "I think I can, I think I can." But other examples of phrases people could use for their personal *holopis*—their private power-summoning affirmation—might include "This is the Olympics," or "Better and better."

mantra (Sanskrit)
Word or syllable uttered to oneself in order to achieve a state of mind; a linguistic mind-tool. [noun]

This word has already begun to enter our language in a rather restricted form: While many Westerners know that *mantra* has something to do with syllables that people chant when they are meditating or performing yogic exercises, few are aware that the word has a more general meaning as *a kind of mental tool.* Just as the Indonesian phrase *holopis kuntul baris* gives people extra muscular strength, many phrases in Sanskrit or Tibetan are said to confer mental states and abilities if they are repeated in the proper manner.

Words have power, just as levers and inclined planes and other tools have power if you know how to use them. And even the least literate human being has access to this power, without knowing where it comes from. Language, in one perspective, is the tool we use to externalize and abstract thoughts; words are tools we use to leverage the power of our minds. And that is precisely what *mantra* means. As we in the West begin to delve into the psychotechnologies of language and uncover the connections between words, beliefs, and power, we might well be able to apply a word like *mantra* in its wider definition.

The Sanskrit prefix *man-* means "think, or have in mind" and is related to the English word *mental.* The Sanskrit suffix *-tra* is used to denote tools or instruments. A *mantra*, then is both literally and figuratively a "mind-tool." In editing *Myths and Symbols in Indian Art and Civilization,* Joseph Campbell, the mythologist and Sanskrit scholar, pointed out this deeper, broader meaning of *mantra* in a footnote:

> Originally the word *mantra* meant simply a verbal instrument for producing something in our minds. Such an instrument was regarded as possessing power. A word or formula—say, "democracy" or "charity"—represents a mental presence or energy; by it something is produced, crystallized, in the mind. The term mantra-'sakti is employed to denote this magic power possessed by words when they are brought together in a formula or effective slogan.

The original meaning also was uncovered by Benjamin Whorf, the anthropologist who revolutionized linguistics through examinations of the links between language, thought, and culture. In his last essay, Whorf wrote:

> The idea, entirely unfamiliar to the modern world, that nature and language are inwardly akin, was for ages well known to various high cultures whose continuity on the earth has been longer than that of Western European culture. In India, one aspect of it

has been the idea of the MANTRAM and of a MANTRIC ART. On the simplest cultural level, a mantram is merely an incantation of primitive magic, such as the crudest cultures have. In the high culture it may have a different, a very intellectual meaning, dealing with the inner affinity of language and the cosmic order.

Now, the old *mantras* are still pretty good—"Aum" and "Om mani padme hum" and "The Lord is my shepherd" still do the job for billions of people—but that doesn't limit the use of linguistic mind-tools to Sanskrit or even to religious terminology. Discovering the true *mantras*—the right combination of words to repeat to oneself in order to find a true path through life—is one of everybody's tasks in life, whether that *mantra* is "Om mani padme hum," "Easy does it," "Thy will be done," "Be here now," "Give me more," "I gotta be me," or "Breathe in, breathe out."

talanoa (Hindi)
Idle talk as a social adhesive. [noun]

People like to talk, whether or not they have anything specific to talk about; in this sense, "idle talk" might be a good candidate for the list of universal human behaviors that pop up in every culture. Although speech is a superb instrument for communicating vital facts, legal and political viewpoints, or artistic truths, it is also a kind of social glue. Anthropologists and linguists are beginning to discover that chitchat, gossip, and idle talk might be more important than we generally think. "Just talking" with someone is a community-building act of communication, even if the content of the conversation is frivolous or "idle." In this way, communities weave their fabric from innumerable strands of otherwise idle conversation. Consider the kind of idle talk that Hindu inhabitants of the village of Bhatgaon in Fiji called *talanoa* (tah-lah-NO-ah), as described by Donald Lawrence Brenneis.

> "Arbitration sessions" and "religious speeches" are part of the larger speech economy of Bhatgaon and must be considered in relationship both to each other and to the range of other available ways of speaking. Both are tightly intertwined with less public communicative events, and particularly with *talanoa*, "idle talk," a principal adhesive in the web of social life in Bhatgaon. While one's general status as an equal derives from sex, age, and residence in the community, specific standing vis-à-vis others is not based on such fixed criteria but comes, in part, from individual accomplishment and, in larger part, from "talk." Here I use "talk" to refer both to the fact of talking with someone and to the contents of conversation. Through conversation one provides accounts and evaluations of people and incidents; by the act of talking one maintains relationships.

What this means in terms of our culture is that we might increase the value we give to mere "talking across the back fence." Water-cooler conversations are important communication channels in many offices—in some, the most important communication channels. *Talanoa*. When you run into a neighbor at the market, take the time for *talanoa*.

haragei (Japanese)
Visceral, indirect, largely nonverbal communication. [noun]

In the West, where we come from a variety of different cultural backgrounds but share the same language, communication is equated with clear, concise, logical, explicit, direct verbalization. Generally, we "speak what is on our minds." On occasion, we "speak from the heart." In Japan, where the culture is racially, socially, and culturally homogenous and people share so many different unspoken values, direct verbal communication the way we use it in the West is generally shunned. Words are mistrusted. Nuances, silences, gestures, facial expressions are much more important. To a surprising degree, the Japanese rely on a kind of visceral communication known as *haragei* (ha-ra-GAY, where the "r" is pronounced something like a "d"). One Japanese can understand what another is trying to communicate by closely observing posture, facial expressions, the length and timing of silences, and the various "meaningless" sounds uttered by the other person.

Indeed, "meaningless" sounds play a large part in *haragei*. Just as Westerners mutter "yes" or "uh-huh" from time to time to indicate intent listening, Japanese tend to say *hai* (hi!). The surface meaning is simply "Yes, I am listening and I hear what you are saying." On a deeper level, *haragei* draws indirect attention to certain nuances of the speaker's words.

One student of Japanese customs, Robert C. Christopher, tells a story of *haragei*:

> Just how addictive *haragei* can be was fully driven home to me a few years ago when a friend of mine, an American journalist long resident in Tokyo, reported on an interview he had just had with one of the elder statesmen of Japan's ruling Liberal Democratic Party. Toward the end of the conversation, my friend asked how many months the politician thought it would be until the then prime minister of Japan would be forced to resign. For his own

reasons, the politician apparently wanted my friend to have the right answer to that question and to publish it. But that posed a problem: The old man clearly felt that with a foreigner, even a knowledgeable foreigner, he could not rely on *haragei*, and yet a lifetime of habit prevented him from giving the answer straight out. In the end, what he did was mutter repeatedly, "*Musakashii ne*" ("a difficult question"), meanwhile using his forefinger to trace very conspicuously on his desktop the number seven.

Although the Japanese raise it to a high art, *haragei* is part of every culture's communication system. In the West, we understand that a sharply raised eyebrow can indicate disapproval, that crossed arms and a grin can indicate aggressive skepticism, that a wink means there are hidden meanings in the speaker's words. But we practice *haragei* far more than we acknowledge it or try to understand it, which means that we sometimes end up with ambiguous understandings.

Njepi (Balinese)
National holiday in which everyone is silent. [noun]

Various religions have sabbath days, during which individuals are enjoined to rest and pray and refrain from working. And a variety of national holidays enable people to take time off their regular jobs in order to jam the highways and crowd the beaches. But what we don't have but could probably use is the kind of holiday the Balinese have in *Njepi* (nn-YEH-pee), their *national day of silence*. The power of words is well known in our society. The power of silence, however, isn't even paid lip-service. Think of what the U.S. might be like if, one day a year, the streets and offices and factories were deserted, the parks and cafés and even kitchens and living rooms were silent!

We will simply never know what we are missing until we all attempt to keep quiet at the same time.

CHAPTER THREE

Dance of the Sexes

Men, Women, and the Words Between Them

Great bodies of knowledge and skill, understanding, and perspective
have had to pass over the millennia from the hands of one sex into the
hands of the other. Otherwise women and men would live in universes
as totally different from each other as those of antelope and grains of
sand. In some societies, in fact, men and women have gone so far as to
speak entirely separate languages.... Within any society men and
women develop differently and have, each, a subculture of their own
that is overbalanced in the importance it places on particular jobs, attitudes, amount of aggressiveness, roles it plays, amounts of expressed
physicality and tenderness, and that has different understandings of
children, of the universe, of the sciences or different access to parts
of the economy, the healing arts, transportation services, and so on....

Judy Grahn, *Another Mother Tongue*

$\mathcal{S}$ex is the most intimate and most volatile forum for
human communication. All of the most intense human dramas of courtship, desire, betrayal, competition, love, friendship, cooperation, deceit, and delusion are wrapped up in the
relations between men and women. From the silent moment
of *mamihlapinatapei* to the bittersweet expression of *razbliuto*

and ultimately to the anguish of *cavoli riscaldati*, male-female relations are fraught with the most intense emotions. With such intensity of feeling and such a potential for deception and miscommunication, the battleground of the sexes is also the spawning ground for many poignant and pointed words. To the degree that clear communication can resolve or prevent conflict, the addition of a few key words to every man's and woman's vocabulary might go a long way toward the negotiation of a mutually amicable covenant.

People in different cultures have differing attitudes toward the physiology of procreation. Subjects that are taboo in one language are objects of casual discussion, or even veneration, in other languages. Many of these words could be metaphorically extended to include phenomena we experience but don't quite understand in contemporary America: In India, *nârâchâstra prayoga* designates a combination of physiology, pornography, and theology, and in Chinese-speaking areas of Asia and the Pacific, the sexually threatening phenomenon of *koro* races through male populations from time to time like a great mental epidemic.

There are words related to female behavior: The German *Torschlusspanik* refers to a kind of anxiety that seems to plague women of a certain age in every culture; the Sanskrit *dohada* refers to a similarly universal female behavior; the Japanese *amaeru* describes one particular kind of woman, while the Yiddish *berrieh* connotes the very opposite. And there are words related to male behavior: The German *Drachenfutter* describes a ritual peculiar to guilty husbands; the Italian *fusto* is applicable only to an especially narcissistic kind of young man; the French *frotteur* can get locked up if he gets caught. Finally, there are words that apply to either gender: The Italian *mettere in piazza* is poignantly applicable to either sex when a certain kind of psychosexual blunder has been committed; the Lakota Sioux *wistelkiya* describes sexual behavior, or lack of behavior, that goes on in every family.

Everybody wants to know what the opposite sex thinks of him or her. And we are all at a loss for words at times, particularly in matters of male-female relationships. The following pages are designed to satisfy some of that curiosity and to provide verbal assistance in those often-vexing communications.

Torschlusspanik (German)
Fear of being left out. [noun]

The direct translation of this expression is "door-shutting panic." It is sometimes paraphrased as "fear of being alone in the park after the gates have been closed for the night." The term is well known in Germany and is used to describe the anxiety that plagues unmarried girls around the age of twenty-one—the fear that they might stay unmarried, and thus unprotected and largely unsupported except by hard labor, for the rest of their lives. In male-dominated societies, which constitute the majority of industrial civilizations and tribal societies alike, a woman's prospects in life are closely related to her marriageability. The male pattern of seeking younger mates in middle age puts heavy pressure on young

women to snag a man as soon as possible or face rapid deval-
uation in the mating marketplace.

A related sensation, perhaps worthy of inclusion in the
wider definition of *Torschlusspanik* (TORE-shloos-pahn-ick),
is the anxiety denoted by the phrase "racing against the biological clock." In the late 1970s and early 1980s, many young
women of the postwar baby-boom generation decided to
delay childbirth. The opening of career opportunities for
women, combined with the advent of modern birth-con-
trol technology, meant that a significant proportion of this
generation delayed the decision to raise a family. But as
these young women reached their late thirties, in the mid
1980s, the onset of *Torschlusspanik* added a new element of
anxiety to the already turbulent realm of contemporary
human mating behavior. Perhaps the most general meaning
of the term in the context of modern America might refer
to any feeling of anxiety regarding sexual competition: "You
have to sympathize with Susan—when she broke up with
Tom and turned thirty-five, she went into a state of full-
blown *Torschlusspanik*."

Although this word has a sharp focus in regard to sexual economics, the metaphor is widely applicable. The way
publishers all seem to produce their own version of a fad
book as soon as one of that category is successful, the idea of
"keeping up with the Joneses," the frenetic search for an
affordable home when mortgage interest rates drop below a
certain level, even the arms race—all are varieties of
Torschlusspanik.

koro (Chinese)
The hysterical belief that one's penis is shrinking. [noun]

Not all epidemics are caused by biological agents like viruses. Some epidemics are psychological, and are spread via rumors and myths. "Dr. Dean Edell's Medical Journal" in the December 12, 1986, edition of the *San Francisco Chronicle* noted the existence of a psychological epidemic that periodically spreads throughout the Far East, sometimes affecting millions of men, whereby the males are convinced that their penises are shrinking into their abdomens, and that if this happens they will die.

Whenever this delusion sweeps across Asia, every decade or two, many men wear bamboo contraptions intended to keep their genitalia from disappearing while they sleep. How could we ever find a use for a word like *koro* (KORE-oh) in Western society? Why would we ever want to? Because it is a perfect metaphor for the way young males of every species seem to act when their mating dance is unsuccessful; *koro* is a perfect word for *male mating behavior that seems to be dominated by some kind of delusory infection.*

This word should be used compassionately rather than pejoratively: In a society where gender roles have been changing rapidly and where a series of severe culturewide psychosexual shocks have detonated within the space of one generation, from the Pill and the sexual revolution of the 1960s and 1970s to the pandemic of sexually transmitted diseases in the 1980s, is it any wonder that men sometimes think their genitalia are shrinking into their abdomens?

With a billion years of biology, half a million years of hunting and gathering, 4000 years of patriarchy, twenty years of women's liberation, all mixed in with frightening new diseases and bombarded every minute by sexually conflicting advertising in every mass medium, the modern American male is an unusually vulnerable candidate for infectious psychosexual hysteria.

You might think of this word as the opposite of *machismo*: Where the macho man tends to believe that he is more "manly" because of his behavior or appearance, the wimpy victim of self-doubts, who may act like a milquetoast or a "sensitive guy" or even as an ersatz macho man, actually believes he is less manly than the norm and fears his masculinity is diminishing as time goes on. When one of your girlfriends begins to decry this form of behavior on the part of someone she knows, turn to her and comment that "It looks like the poor fellow has contracted a case of *koro*." More cruelly, it can be used as a taunt: If some fellow who thinks he is God's gift to womankind and a paragon of virility to be envied by all his buddies happens to make a slip, use this golden opportunity to suggest he might have contracted that terrible new sexual disease—*koro*.

Drachenfutter (German)
Peace offerings for wives from guilty husbands. [noun]

The German custom of *bringing home sweets or flowers for one's wife when one has stayed out late* while "playing poker with the boys" or engaging in other disapproved behavior is probably older and more widespread than anyone realizes. Our species roamed the plains of the world for a hundred thousand years before we settled down to civilization building. During that time, the men were out there hunting, undoubtedly with a little carousing thrown in. But when they returned to their caves, the mighty hunters were in the domain of the women. While they might have wielded the power of life and death over others during the hunt, ancient hunters undoubtedly had to submit to the rulers of the hearth, and may well have felt obliged to make proper propitiations once they returned home.

In Germany, the practice of bringing home chocolates or other gifts was so widespread that it gave rise to the colloquial term *Drachenfutter* (DROCK-uhn-foot-er), which literally means "dragon fodder." At one point it was common in Germany to see men drinking in bars or cafés on Saturday afternoons with their *Drachenfutter* already bought and wrapped in anticipation of the night ahead!

Of course, it is becoming more and more common for women who have their own careers to spend a night out with the girls, and the female version of *Drachenfutter* might become more common. The word can be extended to all gifts or acts that are given or performed out of guilt for having too much fun: Employees give them to bosses, children give them to parents, students give them to teachers. If you catch somebody feeding it to you, or if you are feeling particularly vengeful or simply mischievous, tell your sneaky benefactor that there is a name for that kind of present.

mettere in piazza (**Italian**)
To make intimate feelings or private affairs public. [verb]

In some circumstances, the English phrase "to kiss and tell" is not an adequate description of a verbal indiscretion. What if someone close to you begins to renew a heated argument about a private matter while you are standing in a public place like a subway car or a restaurant? What if you discover that your close friend is telling the world about your secret passion for your next-door neighbor? What can you say when a loved one is on the verge of revealing your embarrassing sexual dysfunction? The Italian phrase for such an *incident in which someone blurts the details of your private life in a public place* is *mettere in piazza* (meh-TEAR-ay een pee-AHT-zah), literally "to put it out in the town square."

This is a particularly good phrase to use if your big-mouthed cohort knows what it means, because it doesn't cause everybody in the vicinity to prick up their ears, the way saying "Don't talk about intimate matters" would. "That's just fine," you might say, when your business partner or loved one begins to spill the beans in public. "Why don't you stop right now before you *mettere in piazza* to no good end?"

Lovers aren't the only ones who engage in this behavior. Don't you hate it when your boss divulges something you told him in confidence, right in the middle of a staff meeting? Kiss-and-tell autobiographies are the publishing world's equivalent. You might say that Joan Crawford's daughter won the prize for literary *mettere in piazza* when she wrote *Mommy Dearest.* In the political realm, infighters behind the scenes often bring embarrassment to their rivals by strategically leaking sensitive information.

razbliuto (Russian)
The feeling a person has for someone he or she once loved but now does not. [noun]

If anything is more ephemeral than life itself, it is that maddening emotion that makes life worth living and that often appears to be beyond mortal control. Entire mythologies and bodies of literature have resulted from the repeated attempts, generation after generation, to answer in prose or pentameter the same old questions about where love came from, where it goes, and why it leaves such bittersweet memories in its wake. The Russian-speaking people give us *razbliuto* (ros-blee-OO-toe) to describe *the feeling a man has for someone he once loved but now does not.*

Of course, since we are adopting the word for our purposes, there is no reason why it should not apply to both sexes. That way, when either a man or a woman faces the painful task of calling the whole thing off, he or she will no longer have to revert to the cliché "I love you, but I'm no longer in love with you." Instead, he or she can sigh, look sympathetic, and say, "I'm sorry, but all I feel about you is *razbliuto.*"

mamihlapinatapei (**Tierra del Fuegan**)
**A meaningful look, shared by two people, expressing
    mutual unstated feelings. [noun]**

The Guinness Book of World Records lists this as "the most succinct word" and defines it as the act of "looking into each
other's eyes, each hoping that the other will initiate what
both want to do but neither chooses to commence."
Whether this is the most succinct word in the world is
arguable, but there is no doubt that the word describes a relatively rare sensation that just about everyone experiences
at some point in life. The eye is both the window of the soul
and the primary erogenous zone; our species was exchanging meaningful glances long before we started compiling
lexicons. And anyone who has ever fallen into love or out
of love, started a fight or ended a fight in such a manner,
knows that the word can apply equally well to any of these
tension-laden situations.

   And here is the answer to precisely what one says in such
a situation: By the very nature of the encounter, it is impossible to simply ask whether the other person has in mind
exactly what you have in mind. But you could always ask if
you both had just engaged in a moment of *mamihlapinatapei*,
and thus approach the matter indirectly. If you want to be
suave about it, you had better spend some time practicing
your pronunciation before you actually try this on someone.
Since it is highly unlikely that a Tierra del Fuegan will be
around to correct you, it is probably better for you to make
up your own pronunciation.

wistelkiya (**Sioux**)
Sexual bashfulness between male and female relatives.
   [noun]

The incest taboo is one of the few beliefs that is shared by virtually all human cultures, no matter how radically they might differ on other important aspects of life. When brothers and sisters and first cousins grow up in close physical proximity, as they did in the tepees of the Plains Indians, close relatives of opposite sexes are expected to observe certain social constraints. Among the Sioux, a man could joke and even flirt with his sister-in-law, but, at least in the old days, was strictly forbidden to even make eye contact with his sister or female cousin. In tribal societies, where inbreeding could wipe out a group in just a few generations, such customs have strong biological justification. The Sioux use the word *wistelkiya* (whistle-KEY-ah) to denote *sexual bashfulness among relatives.*

We might not have a word for it, but the aversion between brothers and sisters is certainly strong in our culture. The commonly accepted and much joked about image of the sibling of the opposite sex, especially in the years before puberty, as a kind of nuisance or even nemesis creates a mock enmity that shields siblings from the conflicting urges they are experiencing. When you notice that your prepubescent children or neighbors are squabbling and avoiding eye contact with one another, you can be sure that *wistelkiya* has something to do with the answer to the age-old question "What got into those kids?"

contre-coeur (**French**)
Against the wishes of the heart. [adverb]

When a person says, "I must have been out of my head when I married him," or "I acted according to my heart, not my head, when I broke up with her," he or she is using a physiological metaphor to make a distinction between those decisions that are made according to the dictates of logic and those that are influenced by feelings or emotions. The French have a specific word for those actions that are taken despite contrary pulls of the emotions, literally "to act against one's heart." You might say that you "acted *contre-coeur*" if you decided to abandon an impoverished lover in order to marry someone wealthy but possibly incompatible. Or you might decide to bet on the sure thing, when you are secretly pulling for the long shot. In France, where the dictates of the heart are taken very seriously, this word has definite pejorative connotations.

Sometimes it is a good thing to act according to the dictates of the heart. At other times (some might say *most* of the time), acting *contre-coeur* is the most prudent course to take. In either case, it probably pays to know the difference, or at least that there is a difference.

fusto (**Italian**)
A man who likes to flex his muscles and dress provocatively.
    [noun]

The orthodox translation of *fusto* (FOOSE-toe) is "barrel," but the colloquial version refers to the kind of man who engages in harmlessly atavistic mating display behavior, found in every human culture and many of the so-called lower species. When this propensity for "dressing up" exhibits itself sartorially, we say that a man is a "peacock." But English doesn't have a suitable word to describe men who *un*dress themselves for public display. *Fusto* is perfect for those occasions when you wonder what to call those young fellows who wear their jogging bikinis to the supermarket or roll their T-shirts up to their shoulder blades, or those not-so-young fellows who leave their shirts unbuttoned to the navel and drape seventeen gold chains across their hairy pects.

Excessive pride in one's physical development, especially if it is more narcissistic than aggressive, is a harmless enough trait, except for that fraction of the *fusto* population whose overdeveloped testosterone level drives them past the borders of mating displays into the hairy competitiveness of male dominance-hierarchies. These fellows love the summertime, but you also see them on ski slopes with their ultratight pants and their perfect form. At their most benevolent, they furnish a symbiotic entertainment at beaches and ski resorts.

The next time the odor of coconut oil is thick in the air and the cushioned clank of gold chains against well-defined chest muscles can be heard from one end of the cabana to the other, turn to your friends and wonder aloud if there isn't a clandestine gathering of *fustos* scheduled for that weekend.

cavoli riscaldati (Italian)
Attempt to revive an old relationship. [noun]

What do you say when an old lover or ex-mate shows up, expecting that you are willing and eager to renew your old relationship? If the relationship ended because your partner was cruel, thoughtless, or unfaithful, these attempts can seem distasteful. If the relationship ended because *you* were cruel, thoughtless, or unfaithful, the attempts can seem equally painful, in an altogether different way. The Italians compare *the attempt to revive a dead love affair* to a cook who tries to reheat old cooked cabbage, a culinary effort that never fails to be unworkable, messy, and distasteful. The Italian phrase for reheated cabbage, *cavoli riscaldati* (KUH-volee ree-skall-DAH-tee), is the appropriate response in this instance: "Tom," (or Laura, as the case may be), "I'm glad to see you, but please, let's not think of continuing where we left off. It would just be *cavoli riscaldati.*"

dohada (Sanskrit)
Unusual appetites or longings of pregnant women. [noun]

According to folk wisdom, if a woman of childbearing age begins to develop sudden cravings for pickles and ice cream, it is time to see the obstetrician. Unusual food cravings, especially if they occur in the middle of the night, are taken as an early sign of pregnancy. This myth seems to be universal: Witness the Sanskrit *dohada* (doe-HOD-uh), a word older than the English language, which refers to these *unorthodox cravings of pregnant women.* Western medicine does not always agree with the tenets of folk medicine, but in this case there appears to be some scientific basis for the ancient folklore, for pregnant women who have unusual cravings (e.g., eating chalk or dirt) have been found to be lacking in certain essential minerals.

If someone in your immediate family remarks that she has developed a strong desire for some salted coffee or curried artichoke hearts, you might want to start thinking about knitting booties.

nârâchâstra prayoga (Sanskrit)
Men who worship their own sexual organ. [noun]

In the battle of the sexes, a nearly universal phenomenon seems to pop up all over the world, in every era and in every culture, whereby the actions of a certain percentage of men seem to be dictated by the needs of their sexual organs. And a smaller percentage of this group seems to regard any actions that bring them genital pleasure as an almost sacred act. In India, the land of a million gods and ten million ways of worshipping, there is a name for phallic obsession that takes on a religious intensity: *nârâchâstra prayoga* (NAH-rah-choz-tra prah-YOE-gah), Sanskrit for the ritual of religious masturbation.

Alain Daniélou, a scholar of the pre-Hindu Shivaite religion, quoting the ancient scriptures known as *Puranas*, describes it thus:

> Some Yogis worship their own sexual organ, that is, the god's presence in themselves. The rite of *nârâchâstra prayoga* (the casting of the dart) [meaning the erection of one's own sexual organ] is carried out by using the thumb and index finger. The votary rhythmically (*japa*) repeats the mantra, *Nanas Shivâya*, and covers his organ with his hand while repeating the *tatpurusha* mantra.... This is called the Hand of Shiva.

The phrase can come in handy for persons of either sex. Women can use it pejoratively, to call a man's attention to his obsessive fixation on genital pleasure. And men can use it as a rationalization for that solitary pleasure they can't seem to keep themselves from indulging in. For the serious meditator who can't seem to escape the bonds of carnal pleasure, it might be an authentic spiritual practice: Say the proper words put yourself in the correct spiritual position, and you can please your Creator as well as yourself.

amaeru (Japanese)
To presume upon another's love, to act like a baby in order to be treated as a dependent. [verb]

In the full Japanese meaning, this word is intimately connected with the meek, dependent role of women in Japanese culture, and particularly the traditional role of women in marital relationships. In some quarters of Western society, this ideal is considered beneficial; others consider it demeaning. For a woman to be *amaeru* (a-ma-EH-roo) is *to be dependent upon the man who loves her, to be protected and cherished.* The way to achieve this state is to pretend that one is less mature, more dependent, more spoiled than one really is. In this sense, the adverb *amae* (AH-may) can refer to various behaviors intended to achieve the state of *amaeru*, as in a tone of voice that is something like a coo, something like a purr, and almost like a whine.

This term transcends male-female relationships and can refer to the behavior of a spoiled child or a pet. In this context, a person may say with pride that a woman is speaking in an *amae* (coquettish) tone, or a child is ingratiating himself to his father. Yet another, more general meaning extends this concept to the general idea of taking advantage of another's kindness, or availing oneself of the hospitality or offer of help proffered by a friend: "I will let myself *amae* of your kind offer" means "I will avail myself of your kind offer."

lingam (Sanskrit)
The symbol of the erect penis as an object of veneration.
   [noun]

In the milieu known as polite society, display of phallic-shaped objects is considered vulgar at best. Polite society, however, is only a recent Western invention. For thousands of years, the symbol of the erect penis was literally worshipped in Asia and the Mediterranean. To this day, you can go to virtually any small village in India and find a shrine to the god Shiva that consists of a penis-shaped sculpture, known as a *lingam* (LEEN-gum), that is usually garlanded with floral offerings. Some might say that the present attitudes toward penis-worship are a modern, and probably ephemeral, aberration.

When the creators of the ancient Hindu religion, the Aryans, invaded India in the 18th century B.C., (around the time that Abraham left Ur to found the Hebrew religion), they found the native inhabitants of the Indian subcontinent worshipping an older god. Shiva was the god of the young, the humble, and of ecology; the protector of animals and trees. His symbol was the erect penis. And his cult was not limited to India, for ample archaeological evidence has uncovered similar sculptures in Corsica and Greece. In ancient Egypt, the sexual organs of Osiris were venerated, and until the 6th century B.C., phallic symbols were worshipped by the followers of Shiva's Mediterranean equivalent, Dionysos.

What is spiritual about the penis? Forty centuries before molecular biologists deciphered the secrets of DNA code, Shivaite worshippers recognized the penis as the organ by which the creative principle manifests itself, and by which the life plan is transmitted from generation to generation. The penis is the visible link between humanity and the creative force that is the basic nature of the divine.

Where the Shivaites saw the penis as a symbol of the divine, Freud saw dream images as penis symbols. When a man or woman dreams of a train entering a tunnel or a spear of asparagus thrusting itself out of the ground, a Freudian analyst won't have any trouble recognizing the symbolism. On the other hand, as Freud himself said, "Sometimes a cigar is just a cigar." If Freud had lived long enough to see the intercontinental missiles, the streamlined shapes of automobiles and airplanes, and the panoply of phallic paraphernalia spawned by 20th-century technological aesthetics, he might have been moved to point out an unconscious resurgence of Shivaism on a global level. In many senses, penis-worship is still the world's most widespread, if unacknowledged, religion.

frotteur (French)
Man who rubs up against strangers in crowds. [noun]

Unfortunately, those men who pay homage to their erections for spiritual purposes are in the distinct minority. One of the hazards of the urban environment are those situations where crowds of strangers are forced to stand very closely together. The subway rush hour, the jammed department store, and other places where stationary, standing crowds can be found are places where a particularly noxious although relatively harmless variety of sexual deviant can be found. The French reserve the word *frotteur* (frawt-HER, with "H" silent) for those individuals who get their jollies by rubbing their crotches against the buttocks of women in crowds. If you ever find this happening to you, chances are you will use stronger language, but if you are in need of law-enforcement assistance, you might consider shouting, "Help! *Frotteur*!"

This word is worthy of extension, for the metaphor implied by this act can encompass all of those acts in which people seek personal pleasure from anonymous, intimate contact with an object of gratification. People who like to rub elbows with the rich and famous, for example, or those *nouveau riche* and just plain tourists who crowd into restaurants where celebrities gather—all represent a kind of non-sexual *frotteur*. The people who crowd into the shot whenever a television camera crew sets up a scene in public are another kind—the media *frotteurs*.

berrieh (Yiddish)
An extraordinarily energetic, talented, competent woman. [noun]

Yiddish was long known as "the mother's tongue," because it was almost strictly spoken by women and passed along from mother to daughter. During the centuries when Eastern European Jews lived in ghettoes and the small towns known as shtetls, the men were expected to be scholarly and study the Torah and converse in either the language of the surrounding country or in Hebrew. While the men took care of important matters, like studying and debating, the women took care of the details of life, like dealing with the landlord, running the household, raising the children, paying the bills. In other words, there was no such thing as "just a housewife" in the old country. When many Eastern European Jews immigrated to the United States, where the man of the family was expected to go out into the world and make a living and the wives were expected to take a secondary role, many women found themselves unduly restricted. As a result, many Jewish women of the first and second generation tended to be "ahead of their time" in terms of taking on roles that had formerly been reserved for men.

As the entire American culture adjusts to the increased importance of women in the workplace, we might adopt the term *berrieh* (rhymes with "dare ya") to describe *a woman with a lot of talent, drive, competence, and a reputation for getting things done.* When your daughter or sister or wife comes home with a promotion, writes an article, organizes a political campaign, or makes a series of brilliant investments, don't tell her she is overstepping her bounds—tell her what a *berrieh* she is.

CHAPTER FOUR

The Eye of the Beholder

Conceptions of Beauty

For the Navajo, beauty is not so much in the eye of the beholder as it is in the mind of its creator and in the creator's relationship to the created (that is, the transformed or the organized). The Navajo does not look for beauty; he generates it within himself and projects it onto the universe.... Beauty is not "out there" in things to be perceived by the perceptive and appreciative viewer; it is a creation of thought.

> Gary Witherspoon, *Language and Art in the Navajo Universe*

Everything that we have so far seen to be true of language points to the fact that it is the most significant and colossal work that the human spirit has evolved.... Language is the most massive and inclusive art we know, a mountainous and anonymous work of unconscious generations.

> Edward Sapir, *Language: An Introduction to the Study of Speech*

$\mathcal{T}$he external environment has obvious effects on language. Less obvious but often more important are the aspects of a culture's *internal* environment that are revealed through the window of language. Although it is rarely visible to us, we each carry around in our heads a conceptual map of the world, a guidebook to rightness and wrongness, ugliness and beauty, value and worthlessness. Strangely enough, your aesthetic guidebook or mine might be completely different from the one carried around by a person who lives a hundred or a thousand miles to the north or south. Just as arctic cultures might include a dozen words for ice, a word that doesn't exist at all in cultures of the Amazon jungle, some languages reveal a cultural focus on concepts that reflect more about people's points of view—the way they see the world—than their surroundings.

The world of aesthetics—beauty in the form of art or exemplified by ideals of human grace—seems to be particularly culture-bound. In one culture, fat women and skinny men are considered to be the paragons of pulchritude. In other cultures, the situation is exactly the reverse. In some countries, everybody is an artist. In other lands, only a small fraction of the population creates art. Some languages are full of words that refer to aesthetic concepts. Other languages are sparse in beauty-related words.

People generally agree that art is more than a collection of marks on paper, or hunks of substance, or people on stage saying words to an audience. The difficulty enters when we attempt to describe what has to be added to endow those marks or hunks or performances with the imprimatur of "art." Without a detailed vocabulary of distinct aesthetic experiences, we are left with a wealth of perceptions that we can *experience* but that we cannot *discuss*—a frustrating situation epitomized by the cliché "I don't know much about art, but I know what I like." In this sense, a little knowledge of the words other cultures use to describe art and beauty can be more than enlightening; it can be useful.

Several of the words in this chapter are Japanese, because the ruling class of Japan at one time concentrated its energies on the refinement of ideas about beauty. Many of the Japanese words for aesthetic concepts and sensations—*wabi, sabi, aware, shibui, yugen*—were developed by members of the Imperial court during the Heian era. The appreciation of beauty, however, is not exclusively an aristocratic trait, or one that can be indulged only by the rich and powerful. On our own continent, the Navajo people of the American Southwest developed an aesthetic that was an essential part of life for every member of the tribe.

Just as the Japanese words for different kinds of beauty can give us a vocabulary for talking about art and about aesthetic feelings, perhaps the Navajo word *hózh'q* can give us an idea of how the creation and appreciation of beauty can be woven in the fabric of daily life. The Navajo attitude toward beauty might be an essential part of what we all have to learn if we plan to navigate this planet into the 21st century in some kind of habitable condition. A revamped global *Weltanschauung*, rather than a web of local perspectives, is a likely requirement for the continued survival of our species, so a new way of looking at life and new ways to live could come in handy for all of us in an eminently practical sense pretty soon. The word *hózh'q* might be a key to this new perspective.

The Chinese *shih* can teach us something about the aesthetics of knowledge, the Russian *ostranenie* can demonstrate how art can literally change the way we perceive the world, the Sanskrit *rasa* and all its variations can give us a detailed vocabulary for describing the effects of art upon the soul, and the Yiddish *kolleh* can remind us that certain people and things are always beautiful—babies, brides, gifts from one's children. By the time you finish this chapter, you will have learned to literally see the world through new eyes.

wabi (Japanese)
A flawed detail that creates an elegant whole. [noun]

If you were to introduce an average American or European to one of Japan's most treasured cultural objects—a teacup made by an old tea-master, for example—very few untrained observers would recognize the *wabi* (rhymes with "bobby") that, to the Japanese eye, distinguishes a museum-quality piece from something a seven-year-old might bring home from art class. Beauty might be in the eye of the beholder, as the old bromide claims, but the eye itself is trained and constrained by the beholder's cultural perspective—everything a person's family, language, and society says explicitly and in many tacit ways about what beauty is and is not. The way individuals perceive "beauty" in other people, the natural world, or human artifacts is profoundly influenced by conscious and unconscious beliefs peculiar to the individual's culture.

To many people who see the world through modern sensibilities, beauty is represented by the kind of technological sleekness, smoothness, symmetry, and mass-produced perfection that is usually associated with a sports car or a skyscraper. A highly prized Japanese teacup, which might fetch tens of thousands of dollars from a collector, might be very simple, roughly fashioned, asymmetrical, and plainly colored. It would not be uncommon to find a crack. The crack—*the beautiful, distinctive, aesthetic flaw that distinguishes the spirit of the moment in which this object was created from all other moments in eternity*—might indeed be the very feature that would cause a connoisseur to remark: "This pot has *wabi*."

To say that we don't have a word for *wabi* in English is not to say that we are incapable of appreciating this kind of beauty. Perhaps more than any other major cultural belief system, aesthetics is *learnable*; that is, people can be trained to recognize beauty where they used to see only flaws. Indeed, the idea of deliberately introducing flaws into works of art is deeply rooted in Western traditions. Because of the biblical injunctions against graven images, all depictions of humans in ancient Jewish sculpture were deliberately flawed. When mechanical weaving machines came along, the distinctive imperfections of Persian hand-woven rugs became hallmarks of quality. As economist Paul Hawken, author of *The Next Economy*, has indicated, it isn't hard to foresee that *wabi*, or something like it, will become increasingly important as our economy changes from a "mass economy," in which wealth is based on large quantities of material resources and energy, to an "informative" economy, based on the design and knowledge built into products and processes.

As the economic conditions that created the "consumer society" change, we seem to be changing our buying habits. One such change is the shift from the goal of owning or consuming a large quantity of possessions or experiences to the goal of owning or consuming a smaller number of *higher quality* possessions or experiences. Some economists call this the "Europeanization" of American buying habits. And one of the consequences of this change in what we perceive as valuable is the return of what used to be called craftsmanship. That's where *wabi* comes in. One-of-a-kind items will grow increasingly more valuable than their mass-produced counterparts. If you want to ride the leading edge of the next inevitable aesthetic wave, look for slightly flawed, wobbly, rustic objects. And when someone remarks about your old piece of pottery or slightly funky wall-hanging, just smile knowingly and say, "Yes, it has *wabi*, don't you think?"

You already know something about *wabi*, but because we didn't have a word for it, you probably didn't think it was important. What about those comfy old shoes or that broken-in, weather-beaten briefcase that seems just perfect to you, even though your spouse is always trying to throw them away? Learning to see the *wabi* in our lives could become an enriching exercise. Everyday life can be art. Living rooms can be art museums. If you learn how to look.

sabi (Japanese)
Beautiful patina. [noun]

Wabi pinpoints a cultural difference of opinion about the relationship between perfection and beauty. In a similar manner, *sabi* (rhymes with "bobby") draws attention to a cultural divergence of opinion about the relationship between age and beauty. Western consumer society (which has strongly influenced Japanese culture in the past few decades) fosters a strong reverence for youth—in appliances and objets d'art as well as people. In Japan, where reverence for one's ancestors is a tenet of the Shinto and Buddhist religions, the situation is reversed: To a Japanese master of rock gardening, an otherwise ordinary rock might be beautiful simply because centuries of moss and lichens have overgrown it in a visually pleasing way. Such a rock would then be said to possess the quality of *sabi*.

It isn't reasonable to expect Americans to have developed much of an appreciation for *the kind of beautiful patina that takes hundreds of years to achieve*. But we have developed our own sense of aesthetic history, suitable to the pace of life here. We don't look back over the centuries, because most of the nation hasn't been here for centuries. But we do look back over the *decades*. One manifestation of this sense of temporal compression is the conversion of fashion into nostalgia. It started in the mid 1970s, when the still-popular aesthetic and cultural nostalgia for the 1960s took hold. In the early 1980s, furnishings and items of clothing from the 1950s became collector's items. As the late 1980s move into the 1990s, nostalgia for the 1970s will undoubtedly have its heyday. So when somebody admires your vintage hand lawn mower or your slightly rusted '52 Chevy, you can say, "Yes, it has a lot of *sabi*."

In Japan, they probably would have decided not to clean off the Statue of Liberty. The act of cleaning certain objects, especially if they have developed a patina that has a beauty of its own, violates the *sabi* of those objects.

aware (Japanese)
The feelings engendered by ephemeral beauty. [noun]

Something of the sweetness and brevity of life is conveyed wordlessly in the fall of a petal. This inspires a kind of awareness known as *aware* (ah-WAH-ray), brought on by that ephemeral, fragile beauty of, say, a cherry blossom as it floats to the ground. Would cherry blossoms be as poignantly beautiful if they bloomed all year round, or if they were as tough as walnuts? Would our worldview be enriched if our notion of beautiful objects expanded to include things that remind us of our mortality?

Whenever somebody sighs because a rainstorm has washed all the petals from a tree, or when the beautiful flower arrangement begins to shed, or whenever something that is beautiful because of its fragility is destroyed by the inevitable passage of time, such is the time to meditate on *aware*. For this word refers not to the external world but to *the human quality of recognizing and feeling these ephemeral, aesthetic aspects of the world.*

Falling cherry blossoms make a beautiful image, but they lack an immediacy for Americans that they have for the Japanese. Nevertheless, anyone who has waxed the car all Sunday afternoon only to watch it rain on Monday knows something about *aware*. Similarly, and somewhat more personally, any man with a magnificent mane who has watched himself getting bald is intimately acquainted with this feeling. Instead of getting angry at rainstorms or creeping baldness, learn to cultivate the bittersweet aesthetic emotion that can arise from contemplation of such phenomena.

shibui (Japanese)
Beauty of aging. [adjective]

Shibui (shin-BOO-ee), like *wabi, sabi,* and *aware,* connotes a certain kind of beauty. Like *sabi,* and unlike *aware, shibui* refers to *a kind of beauty that only time can reveal.* One of the reasons language has such immense emotional power is the way people use symbols to link together several sensory symbols to make an emotionally evocative image. *Shibui* can be used to describe the taste of a certain kind of tea, scenery of a gray, brown, or moss-green color, or the impression a person gets from looking at the face of a certain kind of older person. To a person familiar with Japanese culture and language, these different sensory associations triangulate a distinct but ineffable sensation. To an American, perhaps an analogy can help: Think of Katharine Hepburn's face. She was beautiful as a very young woman. And she grew into a different kind of beauty as age revealed the grain of her character that was hidden beneath the smoothness of her youthful face.

The senses of taste and smell seem to have a strong connection, in all human beings, with memory and time (Proust's *Remembrance of Things Past* was triggered by the taste of a cookie dipped in tea). By linking together the taste of an aged tea, the subdued earth tones of a winter land-scape, and the laugh lines revealed in a human face, this word provokes an emotional as well as a rational reaction. An aged person's face conveys *shibui* to the degree that it reflects the person's personality and his or her experiences in life; thus the remembrance of life's flavors, the reflec-tion of nature's larger cycles of growth and decay, and the psychologically revealing portrait presented by physiog-nomy are combined into one potent, descriptive symbol.

In a worldwide consumer culture where starlets, cosmet-ics, and plastic surgery are industries and social institutions based on the worship of youth, the kind of face that reflects a lot of living is not always valued as it might be in a less youth-oriented realm. Perhaps, as those of the baby-boom generation move into their forties and fifties when the invis-ible sculpturer of time carves their true face from the rela-tively smooth material of youth, a renewed appreciation of this kind of beauty will lead to new attitudes. Next time any-body complains about the ravages of time upon her com-plexion, just tell her that she is beginning to exhibit a delightful *shibui*.

shih (Chinese)
An insightful, elegant kind of knowledge. [noun]

In English, "knowledge" and "wisdom" are roughly differ-entiated into intellectual or spiritual qualities; that is, a scholar or a scientist is expected to have knowledge, and a grandmother or elder statesman is expected to have wisdom. The precise relationship between these two elusively abstract cognitive attributes is a matter of arcane dispute by epistemologists and metaphysicians. In China, where sages and scholars have been the object of reverence for much longer than the English language has existed in its present form, the word *shih* (SHE) indicates a distinction that is part epistemological, part metaphysical, but basically *aesthetic*.

The aesthetics of knowledge are at the heart of several key polarities in the history of Chinese thought. The kind of knowledge that anyone can gain by studying is called *hsüeh* ("book learning" would be the closest equivalent). A person can possess a wide and deep knowledge of factual material, but unless that person has a kind of *insight, judgment, and above all good taste in the way that this knowledge is used or presented*, that person cannot be said to possess *shih*.

In the Western world, mathematicians regularly apply aesthetic terms like *beautiful* or *elegant* to ideas or knowledge. Perhaps as the English-speaking culture matures, we will begin making the same kind of fine distinctions in everyday speech that only literary critics and aestheticians make today. Sports fans and dance aficionados know all the nuances to describe the difference between a spectacular physical feat and a spectacular physical feat that was performed with special grace, style, and form. Olympic gymnastic judges know the difference between flawless but uninspired performance and one that combines technical expertise with *shih*. A person who goes into a French country restaurant, turns to the waiter (who is also the cook), and says, "The wild mushrooms should be good this time of year," even though they aren't on the menu, is exhibiting a kind *shih.* This special elegant wisdom is acknowledged by the waiter/cook when he smiles and says, "Leave it to me, monsieur."

We can all help hasten the day when insight becomes a desirable kind of beauty, along other important aesthetic criteria, like possessing a good head of hair, fashionably arranged musculature, or a pretty face. We can single out and acknowledge *shih* when we see it, instead of devoting all our epistemological attention to the raw accumulation of *hsüeh.*

rasa (Sanskrit)
The mood or sentiment that is evoked by a work of art.
   [noun]

Close your eyes, twist a piece of orange peel under your nose, and inhale deeply. That sensation is what the Hindu inhabitants of India would call the fruit's *rasa,* or essence. In a literal sense, the word refers to the essential oils of a fruit or the perfume of a flower. But it is also used to describe something many cultures don't have the words to describe: *the thrill of aesthetic pleasure, powerful emotional resonance, and mood or sentiment evoked when a person experiences a work of art.* Effective use of this word could remedy an occasion for social awkwardness in our culture: What do you say to your companion as you gaze at a painting or after you attend an inexplicable performance piece?

One of the reasons why "art" is so hard to define is that

it is a matter of subjective judgment, arising from the psychological (and thus only indirectly observable) effect the work has on the people who view it or hear it. Sanskrit, the language of the great yogis and other psychotechnologists of ancient Asia, includes a rich choice of words for describing aspects of the inner life of experience. The full theory of *rasas* lays out an aesthetic vocabulary for describing the "essences" of very different kinds of work.

For more than 1500 years, Hindus have acknowledged nine distinct *rasas* at least one of which will be present in any work of art. The erotic *rasa*, *Shringara*, a frequent theme in Indian art, evokes powerful responses in viewers by rendering the beauty of the human body or by portraying familiar emotions, such as the passionate longing experienced by separated lovers. The comic *rasa*, *Hasya*, epitomized by incongruous situations and unexpected juxtapositions, can be applied even to the gods: A sculpture of the beloved, rotund, elephant-headed god Ganesha depicts the ungainly figure in the pose of Shiva performing his delicate dance. *Karuna*, the pathetic *rasa*, evokes feelings of despair, similar to the realization of permanent separation that accompanies the death of a loved one. *Raudra*, the furious *rasa*, is depicted by paintings, plays, and sculpture of the Hindu panoply of demon hordes and wrathful deities, engaged in eternal combat. The selfless heroes who express the dignity and higher spirituality of gods and mortals are often the subjects of art based on *Vira*, the heroic *rasa*. The evocation of fear is the realm of the terrible *Bhayanaka rasa*. To the vegetarian Hindus, the quintessence of the odious *Bribhatsa rasa* would be a painting of a man eating the raw heads of various animals. The supernatural surprises that greet the heroes of legends are the focus of the marvelous *rasa*, *Adbhuta*, and the serenity known only by those who turn away from the world of the senses is the topic of the tranquil *Shanta rasa*.

If you seek a frame of reference to describe the feeling you carry away from an experience of Beethoven's Ninth or van Gogh's *Starry Night* or Tennessee Williams's *A Streetcar Named Desire*, *rasa* is the word for you. If you want to venture into the realm of the impressive and skirt the border of the pretentious, you can always remark that the X-rated drama "reeked of *Shringara rasa*," or the cool jazz concert "evoked the *Shanta rasa* in me."

hózh'q (Navajo)
The beauty of life, as seen and created by a person. [noun]

Quick—think about your wealth. You probably thought about your bank balance, stock portfolio, real estate, or other economic measures. If you were to ask the same question of a Navajo, you might discover that your informant's reaction is to count the number of songs he or she knows, especially the ones self-created. Which of those answers is the more sophisticated? To the Navajo, *beauty is not only a way of looking at life, but is in itself a way to live.*

One clue to what we need to add to our worldview is the fact that the word *beauty*, to most people, is more likely to be associated with frailty and ornament than with power and substance. The worldview that sees a redwood forest as a potential parking lot with lumber on it is founded on an illusory split between humans and the world in which we exist. In many societies, including our own, beauty is seen as a peripheral aspect of life, while the instrumental aspects of business, politics, and technology are seen as the central, "real" concerns of life. To the Navajo, however, who lived in an often hostile environment that required the most practical concerns, the creation and appreciation of beauty is strongly tied in with the economic, emotional, and intellectual well-being of the ordinary individual living his life.

To the non-Navajo mind, beauty is a quality that is abstracted from the surfaces of things: We see beautiful apples or hear beautiful symphonies. To the Navajo, beauty is the entire gestalt of perceiver, apple, symphony, society, religion. In that way, *hózh'q* (HOE-shk) is like the Chinese word *tao*; *hózh'q* is simply the way the universe ought to be. But while the *tao* is the *tao* whether we see it or not, *hózh'q* is something that grows from within a human being and spreads outward to permeate the universe. In this passage from *Language and Art in the Navajo Universe*, Gary Witherspoon underlines the generative connotations:

> In the Navajo world, where mind and matter, thought and expression are inseparably connected, the aesthetic experience—the creation of beauty—is simultaneously intellectual, emotional, moral, aesthetic, and biological. Navajo life and culture are based on a unity of experience, and the goal of Navajo life—the creation, maintenance, and restoration of *hózh'q*—expresses that unity of experience. *Hózh'q* expresses the intellectual concept of order, the emotional state of happiness, the moral notion of good, the biological condition of health and well-being, and the aesthetic dimensions of balance, harmony, and beauty.

Tell your friends about *hózh'q*, and when you hear people boasting about their salary or their new boat, tell them about how many new songs, paintings, poems, or flower arrangements you created last year. When they look at you as if you've gone daft, smile knowingly and explain that you've been practicing *hózh'q* in your daily life.

ostranenie (Russian)
Art as defamiliarization; making familiar perceptions seem strange. [verb]

Is art something that makes life enjoyable? A way for non-conformists to make a living and affirm their identities? A rest-and-recuperation tool for hardworking people? Or is it an essential part of human culture? These questions have probably been debated since the first cave-dwellers started daubing vegetable dyes on their walls. And they will undoubtedly be the cause for discussion when our descendants make art on other planets. According to at least one school, the Russian formalists, the purpose of art is to "defamiliarize" the world. The word *ostranenie* (ohsh-truh-NYEHN-yay), used in this sense, means *the "making strange" of objects and perceptions that are familiar.* In this sense, art has profound psychological and cultural functions. Indeed, without "crazy artists" to make the familiar seem strange, we might still be huddled in our caves, waiting for the hunters to return with some raw meat to get us through the night.

On the psychological level, people learn how to cope with the world by making the many perceptions we encounter into familiar objects. We build models of the world out of our perceptions, then tend to project that model onto the world, ignoring new details and odd nuances that don't fit in with what we have come to expect. On the cultural level, it is difficult to make progress in a world that is constantly being familiarized. Where does innovation come from, for example? In this sense, *ostranenie* is a vital function of art, for it breaks us out of our normal ways of seeing and thinking and creates the possibility of seeing and thinking in new ways. While habituation and familiarity are necessary psychological tools for creating an orderly world, they can grow into prisons that keep us from seeing the unusual, the marvelous, the might-have-been and ought-to-be. And then a van Gogh, a Picasso, a Stravinsky, a Joyce, or a Cervantes comes along and turns all our familiar ideas upside down.

In educational policy debates, *ostranenie* ought to be raised as one powerful answer to the question of why art ought to be taught along with such essential subjects as reading, writing, and arithmetic. And in several senses, this word ought to be used in our internal dialogues, our conversations with ourselves. The familiarization of the world is an all-too-common phenomenon in an age when you can travel to virtually every major city in every country and stay in the same kind of room that is part of the same hotel chain, eat the same fast food, and watch the same television shows. But the defamiliarization of the world, the renewal of perceptions, is necessary for our mental well-being. Artists can show us the way, to the extent of actually changing our perceptions. Would your feeling about the sunlight on a poplar on a summer day be the same if you had never seen a Monet? And would those flashy computer-generated television commercials capture your attention and imagination if they didn't show us how familiar objects can be seen in entirely new ways?

Ostranenie can be a perceptual cleansing tool. As poet William Blake put it, if our "doors of perception" were to be cleansed, we would see the world as it really is: infinite. So when somebody asks why you are staring at that poplar tree or why you seem fascinated with the white noise between radio channels, tell them that a little *ostranenie* can make the familiar seem marvelous.

yugen (Japanese)
An awareness of the universe that triggers feelings too deep and mysterious for words. [noun]

"To watch the sun sink behind a flower-clad hill, to wander on and on in a huge forest without thought of return, to stand upon the shore and gaze after a boat that disappears behind distant islands, to contemplate the flight of wild geese seen and lost among the clouds." American philosopher Alan Watts used the words of a Japanese poet to describe a sensation that, by its nature, lies beyond the power of words. "All these are *yugen*," Watts notes, "but what have they in common?"

Yugen (YOO-gehn, with a hard "g") is an extension of *aware*, an opening of aesthetic perceptions to include the vastness and ultimate fragility of the universe itself. Where *aware* is a sensation triggered by confrontation with evidence of the brevity of life, *yugen* carries the sensation into the realm of mystery, for the essence of Zen is an awareness that "all form is void," that the universe itself is an ephemeral object. Such an awareness is too deep for the kind of aesthetic categories that govern ordinary art. It cannot be depicted, only suggested. *Aware* is a pleasant sensation, triggered by the generally unpleasant thought of mortality. *Yugen* springs from an awareness that even *aware* is ephemeral. It is *the sense of unutterable depth and profundity* that sets *yugen* as a boundary on language: Poetry cannot explicitly state, but can only suggest, the unendurable, indescribable poignancy of the sensation that is named, but not described, by the word *yugen*. The famous Japanese haiku often evoke *yugen*.

If you want to experience the feeling suggested by this word, sit on a cliff alone, at sunset. When the last rays of the sun have died and night begins to fall, when the chill begins to soak into your bones, wait for the first mournful cry of the birds, and note the sensations you feel. When your spouse walks up and asks you what you are thinking, you can say, "I'm not thinking, my dear. I'm feeling *yugen*."

kolleh (Yiddish)
A (beautiful) bride. [noun]

Feminine beauty is a cultural concept. In contemporary America, beauty is so strongly identified with thinness that many young women suffer from eating disorders as a result of their efforts to achieve desirable results. In other countries and other cultures, a thin woman is considered highly undesirable, and various kinds of "fattening butters" are urged upon these unfortunates.

In every culture, there are many who do not fit the current standards of beauty, and this can cause a great deal of grief to the person who is considered homely because of the way her nose tilts or doesn't tilt, or the amount of subcutaneous body fat or lack of it on her hips or other parts of her body. This matter of aesthetic standards once caused an ethical controversy among pious Jews, who considered it sinful to lie. If one is always to tell the truth, what do you tell the parents and groom of a homely bride? The great scholars whose judgments were collected in the Talmud addressed their efforts to this theological, ethical, and aesthetic question. A student of the great Rabbi Hillel wrote the line that became an established part of Talmudic doctrine: *"Every bride is beautiful and graceful."*

You don't have to be Jewish to adopt this attitude. It isn't a legalism. It happens to be true, at least in the eyes of the groom. And everybody else ought to make an effort to see her through her husband's eyes, at least on the one day of her lifetime when it matters the most. The Yiddish word *kolleh* (KOLL-eh, rhymes with "Walla Walla") means "bride," and is an appropriate word to use when you want to show someone how to recognize that certain circumstances grant a kind of beauty to a person that transcends conventional aesthetic notions. It doesn't have to be limited to brides. Every mother's baby is beautiful. Every child's puppy is beautiful. And that lumpy ashtray that your child brings home from summer camp is certainly *kolleh*.

CHAPTER FIVE

Serious Business

Words About Work and Money

Without some dissimulation, no business can be carried out at all.
Philip Stanhope, Earl of Chesterfield, 1749

*N*othing's more serious than business, no matter where you go in the world. And nothing can be funnier than some of the terms and customs that have grown up around economic activity. Business is a quintessentially social activity and thus is flavored by several key human traits, such as humor, irony, and pathos. When two opposing business leaders go head to head on Wall Street, they do it with hostile takeovers, junk bonds, and attorneys. When they do it in the Trobriand Islands, they use a particular ritual that one anthropologist noted produced more fear and anxiety than any other public event she had witnessed. Wait until you find out what common household object the Trobrianders use to mediate economic conflict.

The factory, office, or workplace is where most people spend most of their time, so it is only to be expected that humorous or cynical terms and phrases will emerge from these environments. The Italians pay homage to a specific kind of finely crafted creative goldbricking in their word *ponte* and call those who are adept at building them *pontisti*. Everyone in your office knows what a *ponte* is, and everybody knows who your local *pontisti* are. Now you'll have a word for it. The worldview of the Italian pragmatist is amply demonstrated by the word *bustarella*, an unofficial, ubiquitous, and delicate business act that is known everywhere in the world. And the Italian phrase *tirare la carretta*, which literally means "to pull the little cart," is at once a joke and an existential reflection on the nature of work. Anybody who works for somebody else will instantly understand why Germans have an unflattering word, *Radfahrer*, for people who behave in a certain way to fellow workers, and a downright insulting word, *Korinthenkacker*, for people who are overly concerned with trivial details. And everyone who has been the victim of a certain specific and particularly painful variety of bungling will appreciate the French epithet *gâchis*.

The Dutch word *plunderbund* lays it right on the line about capitalism, and the Polish word *fucha* describes an activity that thrives clandestinely under socialism. The Spanish word *gajes* is applicable to a particular range of items not included on a job description. The Yiddish term *aroysgevorfeneh gelt* poignantly describes an especially painful variety of bad investment. The French even have the expression *faux frais* to describe one of the illusions of budgeting.

Perhaps most important, there are words that show how other cultures have elevated graceful salesmanship to an art, demonstrated the psychological finesse required for inspired management, or who have turned both capitalism and socialism inside out by creating status through the act of dispersing rather than accumulating or redistributing wealth. In direct contradiction to the "lifeboat ethics" of "all is fair in love, war, and business," the French *lagniappe* refers to a kind of salesmanship that would have appalled Ebenezer Scrooge. The Japanese process of *nemawashi* shows how a leader can make decisions by considering the communications that occur *before* a meeting. The Haida word *potlatch* describes a ceremony that is an astonishing parody of capitalism. And the Trobriand Islander, with *kula*, turns the process of gift-giving into a sacred, endless cultural process.

By the time you have added all the words in this chapter to your vocabulary, you will be exceedingly well equipped to deal with the pragmatic, the theoretical, the ironic, and even the spiritual side of business. Indeed, when it comes to the invisible social infrastructure of economic activity, many MBAs will get more of a business education from this chapter than they ever received in business school. As an additional bonus, there is even one word—*bricoleur*—that can be used to explain the mess in one's office.

bricoleur (French)
A person who constructs things by random messing around without following an explicit plan. [noun]

Are you the kind of worker, decision-maker, designer, artist, businessperson, or engineer who builds a detailed plan for each creation, then follows it, step by step? Or do you just start pottering around with ideas or materials until some kind of order begins to emerge? If you are the latter kind of worker, you've probably suffered the jibes and innuendos of your more analytically minded colleagues, and if you are any good at "thinking by the seat of your pants," you also know that you are capable of putting together concoctions on the fly that the careful preplanners will probably never achieve in years of deliberate effort. Take heart, *bricoleurs*, for French anthropologist Claude Lévi-Strauss has given you a word to use with pride.

Lévi-Strauss, in describing the way "primitive" cultures approach theory-building in their empirical disciplines, used the term *bricolage* as a model for the way all humans, "primitive" or "civilized," build scientific theories by "pottering around" with natural objects in various combinations. A *bricoleur* in this sense is *a kind of intuitive technician who plays with concepts and objects in order to learn about them.* The word was picked up by the American computer scientist and educational expert Seymour Papert, one of the creators of Logo, a computer language designed to help children think more effectively. In his book *Mindstorms,* Papert points out how the terms can extend to an entire way of thinking:

> The process reminds one of tinkering; learning consists of building up a set of materials and tools that one can handle and manipulate. Perhaps most central of all, it is a process of working with what you've got. We're all familiar with this process on the conscious level—for example, when we attack a problem empirically, trying out all the things that we have ever known to have worked on similar problems before. But here I suggest that

> working with what you've got is a shorthand for deeper, even
> unconscious learning processes.... Here I am suggesting that in
> the most fundamental sense, we, as learners, are all bricoleurs.

The next time somebody suppresses a smirk at your messy desk or your disorganized manner of attacking a problem, just smile punctiliously and say, "I guess I'm just a *bricoleur* at heart, my friend!"

bustarella (Italian)
A euphemism for a cash bribe. [noun]

Bribery has been an essential lubricant in business deals ever since commercial transactions were invented, especially those that involve procuring licenses from low-paid functionaries. In fact, bribery is on the short list of universal human traits, along with language, the incest taboo, and taxation. In many countries, both the public and the government expect some public officials to accept *low-level bribery* as part of the benefits they receive from their work in lieu of a decent salary. But it is unethical and criminal and frowned upon (publicly) in America, so we really haven't developed an eloquent English euphemism for suggesting that a cash bribe would be the solution to certain obstacles.

The Italian *bustarella* (boost-ah-REH-lah) is a diminutive of the word for "envelope." Doesn't "little envelope" sound elegant? No need to mention the contents. Here are several suggested uses: "The special terms of the contract are specified in the *bustarella*." "I understand that this licensing procedure can be expedited with a *bustarella*." "I think I know how to solve your problem, but we will have to pass around a *bustarella* or two."

biritilulo (Kiriwina, New Guinea)
Comparing yams to settle disputes. [noun]

The difference between literal and metaphorical meaning of words and gestures is most critical when it comes to the rites and rituals we use to mediate conflicts between people. In the Trobriand Islands, settling disputes between different social groups can be a thorny matter, even in a racially and culturally homogeneous society like that of the Kiriwina, who believe that people can live together in peace only if nobody talks about what everybody knows concerning certain sensitive matters. Because of taboos built into their use of language, opposing Kiriwina individuals and groups can find themselves involved in mortal combat if they happen to say the wrong thing in the heat of anger. (See *mokita* and *biga peula* in chapter two.) In order to avoid or defuse the potentially explosive situations, the Kiriwina resort to a linguistic abstraction involving an inanimate object that has great symbolic importance in Kiriwina life and lore—the yam.

Anthropologist Annette B. Weiner, who lived among the Kiriwina, wrote, "A *biritilulo* [bury-tee-LOO-low] produces more fear and anxiety than any other public event I witnessed." This fearsome ritual occurs when two opposing clans gather in front of witnesses, then retire for a short time and produce a number of yams, which are then exhibited and compared against one another! To understand the way this culture has found a way to use such a seemingly innocuous object as an important social pressure valve, it is necessary to understand the central importance of yams to Kiriwina life and society. Each adult male in the society owns a yam house, which is filled not by the individual's unassisted efforts but through the work of all the men who are related to the owner by means of a network of kinship and clan connections. During the yam harvest, men spend most of their time working for other men.

Because the yam is a currency and a symbol of important social relationships, the act of displaying a yam is a potent means of drawing attention to the power, abilities, status, or political intentions of the person or group who displays it. When a member of a group makes the mistake of saying the irrevocable "hard words" (see *biga peula* in chapter two) to a member of another group, the individuals and their associates have the choice of combat or the ritualistic comparison of yams. The offending individual's clansmen quickly organize a *buritilulo*; as soon as the loud and frightening but ultimately harmless exchange of boasts about the size of the opposing clan's yams is under way, fighting is averted.

In contemporary American business practices similar situations sometimes arise, in which people watch their colleagues drift toward mutually destructive infighting and outright conflict, often over an incident where one party or the other made the mistake of saying some "hard words." In politics, these disputes are sometimes handled informally, by the opposing politicians' clans of advisers. In business, a ritual for averting conflict is badly needed. On the international level, wouldn't it be a powerful tool for peace if we could only convince diplomats to use yams instead of armies to settle arguments? The next time you see your boss or your colleague on a collision course, and you are on friendly terms with a friend of the opposing side, perhaps you ought to suggest an Americanized version of *biritilulo*: Gather at the local bar and select a ritual object for clamorous comparison: A personal computer? Briefcases? Watches?

potlatch (Haida)
The ceremonial act of gaining social respect by giving away wealth. [noun/verb]

The Haida (Native American) word *potlatch* (POT-latch) neatly reverses normal conceptions of how business ought to be conducted and reveals the close connection between shared social values and the fundamentals of economic activity. The idea that the spiritual benefits of exchanging goods might exceed the material benefits is one worth considering in this age when so many people seem to "know the price of everything and the value of nothing." Price is a means of measuring the way a market behaves in response to the supply and demand of a product or service, but value is a matter of cultural agreement and deeply held, often unconscious individual beliefs. And that is why it is possible to create a society in which people can gain value by giving something away.

In industrial and preliterate societies alike, the main idea behind "doing business" is to get as much for yourself, usually at the expense of others: You can seize wealth through war or banditry, or you can induce people to exchange part of their wealth for your skills or materials. As your wealth increases, through your skill and luck in economic transactions, so does your social status. "Getting ahead" in the eyes of such societies is directly correlated with the size of one's bank account, whether the currency consists of yams or Eurodollars. Among the native tribes of the Oregon, Washington, and Canadian coasts, however, where the resource-rich environment made sustenance easier than it was for inhabitants of less hospitable locales, the notion of "getting ahead" in the eyes of society was linked to one's propensity for *giving away* wealth!

The Westerners who first encountered a Haida *potlatch*—a word that denotes a ceremony, a process, and a way of looking at life—were astonished to see one clan working year-round to prepare for *a stupendous feast in which all the guests were sent home with valuable gifts*! As R. R. Marett, an early anthropologist, described it:

> The "potlatch" or distribution feast of the northwest coast of America is on face of it a display of reckless prodigality, inasmuch as the clan that gives entertainment strips itself bare of its property in order to send away its guests loaded with complimentary gifts. Did it stop here, they would have lost everything except honour. It is incumbent on the visitors, however, unless they would be disgraced, to hold similar feasts in due course, so as to repay the favours shown them with no less prodigal interest. Yet it is surely a noble form of rivalry not to be outdone in generosity rather than in the art of snatching a profit.
>
> So too, then, all over the savage world the prime function of most of the ceremonial giving and taking is to betoken mutual regard and a readiness to share as is proper among friends. . . .

Modern commerce might well borrow from its old-world prototype something of that non-calculating, non-competitive spirit which proclaims getting to have little or no value apart from giving.

To the Haida, partying was a means of distributing wealth, and they did not party to celebrate fulfilling a social contract but rather *maintaining* it. To the Haida, the road to greatness was not through war or conquest, but through great *potlatching*. The white people who conquered the Northwest were morally outraged by these wild gift-giving parties and outlawed them. In our own time, the egregious displays of wealth at parties where thousands of dollars worth of ice sculpture and party favors for the guests are displayed, the word is applicable in its darkest sense. The party thrown by the late Shah of Iran to celebrate Persia's 2500th anniversary was notorious for the splendor of the gifts carried away by guests—and was one of the factors that led to his downfall.

But the dark side of *potlatching* comes into play only when the practice becomes a toy for a ruling elite. For the masses, it might not be a bad idea. Some would say that if we ever hope to achieve utopia, we need to integrate ideas like this into our daily thinking. At the very least, we owe it to our future to try it out in case it works. Be the first on your block to *potlatch*: Throw a lavish party, give away everything you own, and if your friends don't have you committed to a mental institution, remind them enthusiastically that you are looking forward to *their potlatches* in reciprocation.

kula (Trobriand Islands)
Sacred, endless process of gift-giving. [noun]

A person's net worth or a nation's gross national product are quantitative but static measures of wealth. Another way to measure the economic health of a community is to look at the places financial tokens *circulate*, rather than concentrating on where they accumulate, and more importantly, the way in which the circulation of currency forces people to interact with one another. In the industrial world, capitalists and socialists alike know that you get ahead in the world by adding more dollars or rubles or yen to your bank balance than you subtract. Another thing that people in currency-using economies agree upon is that bank balances, coins, paper money, and electronic transactions are symbols for other kinds of wealth—arms, food, heavy machinery, works of art.

The great seafaring traders of the Trobriand Islands, however, demonstrated that it is possible to value currency in a very different way, and to engage in *a kind of commerce that is truly symbolic, involving the exchange of cultural information rather than goods and services.* The *kula* (KOO-lah), an endless, circular series of ceremonial gift-givings between groups of men spread out over many different islands, is the name for the custom that occupies perhaps half the life of Trobriand men. The pioneering anthropologist Bronislaw Malinowski, in his *Argonauts of the Pacific,* compared and contrasted these Trobriand seafarers with the Greek heroes who sailed in search of the Golden Fleece. Just as the West-

ern Argonauts were after the Fleece for its magical properties (and for the glory of the quest), their Pacific counterparts were "in the *kula*" for life, and considered it a high
privilege and sacred obligation.

In every island and village of this culture, a certain limited number of persons were privileged to take part in a constant cycle of exchange, in which white-shell armlets were
given from person to person in one navigational cycle, while
red-shell armlets were distributed in the opposite directions.
Prodigious feats of seafaring were required, which in turn
necessitated the maintenance of detailed knowledge of the
stars, sea, and weather patterns. Each object that was given
was named, and its personal history was learned by each
recipient, to pass along to the next temporary custodian.
The satisfaction gained by the "owner" of currency would
lie in the recitation of the object's history in the *kula*.

America's use of automobiles, electronic entertainment
equipment, and a thousand other "status symbols" indicates
a cultural willingness to engage in semiotic intercourse. All
we need to do is convince enough people that true status
can be gained by passing wealth around in the form of useful information, rather than hoarding or flaunting it in the
form of symbolically important material objects.

Korinthenkacker (German)
A person overly concerned with trivial details. [noun]

Every law office has the person who takes up hundreds of
dollars of billable time at meetings reminding people not to

waste yellow pads. And everyone has experienced the nit-picking enthusiasm of a calculator-wielding lunch partner who insists upon finding the exact amount owed by each of eight people rather than splitting the tab eight ways. Perhaps it was because of the connection between toilet training and subsequent peculiarities of adult attitudes toward money that Sigmund Freud hypothesized, under the label of "anal-retentiveness," that nitpickers of the extreme variety tend to fixate on monetary matters. But financial trivia, unfortunately, do not constitute the sole domain of these bores, whose focus is always on the detail and never on the big picture. Even worse, in the opinions of some people, are the rules freaks, who have memorized *Robert's Rules of Order* and use their knowledge to no better end than turning each meeting into a parliamentary debating nightmare.

The German language has a compound word for people overly concerned with the petty, inconsequential details in life, often at the expense of more important matters. The word *Korinthen* is the plural of "raisin," and *Kacker* is a relatively polite term for a person engaged in an act of bodily elimination. (German scatology can be much more harsh than this, especially when vile personal habits are described in terms of excretory metaphors.) So, while "raisin-crapper" might be the direct translation, the meaning of the term *Korinthenkacker* (core-IN-ten-COCK-er) is meant to be broad enough to include *anyone who couldn't find a forest because he or she is too busy applying a magnifying glass to an inspection of the bark of one tree.*

Radfahrer (German)
One who flatters superiors and browbeats subordinates. [noun]

Although the literal translation of this is "cyclist," it colloquially refers to the kind of *obsequious martinet who fawns over
anyone of higher rank*, or anyone who might conceivably do
the *radfahrer* (RAHD-far-ur) any good, then turns around
and browbeats subordinates. The term's precise meaning is different from sycophant, for the sycophant's energies are
truly concentrated on winning the favor of superiors, where
the *Radfahrer* adds the despicable twist of turning around
and abusing subordinates. Every organization, whether it is
a multinational corporation or a church parish in a small
town, has one of these. And every culture, from Mesopota-
mia to Manhattan, has undoubtedly harbored its quota of
these specimens whose motives are transparent to everyone but themselves. The Germans named this odious type,
but there's no reason why their contemptuous word should-
n't be more widely adopted.

faux frais (French)
**Items you are likely to forget to include when making a
budget. [noun]**

Here's a problem that vexes small households and sover-
eign nations: figuring out in advance how you are going to
spend your money. No matter how thoroughly you do your
research, how conscientiously you build in fudge factors,

how hard you work at sticking to a prearranged budget, doesn't it seem as if you always end up outspending your target amount, especially if it is an annual budget? How does this happen? Did you remember to include the cost of replacing a cracked windshield or removing an impacted wisdom tooth? Life is an illusory raft on an ocean of uncertainties. How can you ever anticipate all the expenses that can possibly pop up in the course of a year? The French have a word for it. Whenever you have to explain why your expenses are 150 percent greater than your forecast, just shrug your shoulders and say, "There must have been an unusually high incidence of *faux frais* [foh-FRAY] this year."

For those who believe in the creative extension of language, the term could be expanded to include anything that you forgot to pack or plan for or buy. We need a phrase for minor instances of lapsed foresight, and a French term helps distance us from our own forgetfulness. The absence of a jack in your car could be interpreted as a *faux frais*. Similarly, while you are likely to remember to bring suntan lotion when you go to the beach, you may well encounter the *faux frais* of having forgotten to pack sunburn cream.

gâchis (French)
Strong epithet for an opportunity-bungling mess caused by ineptness. [noun]

For all those who have ever wondered, while steam vented from your ears, what to call the mess that an especially talented bungler can create, and for all those who have watched inept partners, subordinates, or bosses *blow important opportunities through sheer disorganization and fuzzy thinking,* here's a word for you. Unless the person who managed to discard the major contract in the trash or flub the important product demonstration by forgetting to bring spare parts happens to be your boss or a close relative of the boss, you can now tell him or her to "take your fine *gâchis* (gah-SHE) out of here."

French has separate words for messiness, disorder, and stupidity, but *gâchis* is reserved for those rare and poignant circumstances where a talent for these entropic traits meets a situation where bungling of awe-inspiring proportions can ruin a truly sweet deal. Unfortunately, it is a common word, and usage cuts across all boundaries of nation, age, race, gender, and class.

ponte (Italian)
An extra day off, taken to add a weekend to a national holiday. [noun]

The great thing about national holidays is that a large proportion of the population stays home from work. And when the holiday comes on a Friday or a Monday, the great national pastime known as the three-day weekend lightens the routine for millions of workers. Unfortunately, holidays sometimes fall on Tuesdays or Thursdays. In every office and factory, however, a certain percentage of the workforce manages to arrange a personal day off or a sick day to combine holiday and weekend into a four-day vacation.

The Italians, who love this practice as much as anybody else, use their word for bridge, *ponte* (PONE-tay), to describe this practice. When you arrange a crucial, all-day dentist appointment for Friday when New Year's Day is a Thursday, you might be said to be "building a *ponte*." Because this is such an obvious day for *pontes*, many managers and supervisors make it less than easy to construct them. Nevertheless, there is always a motivated and talented cadre of *ponte*-builders who manage to find a way. The Italians call these experts *pontisti* (pone-TEES-tee).

This word could slip right into our language with hardly any adjustment. "I'm building a *ponte*," you can say on Wednesday afternoon before a Friday holiday, and everyone will know what you mean as soon as you call in sick on Thursday. When you run into a friend at the beach on a Monday before a Tuesday holiday, you can both shrug and say, "I guess we're both *ponting* today."

nemawashi (Japanese)
Informal feeling-out and consensus gathering. [verb]

American business leaders have been falling all over themselves to adopt Japanese management techniques and to read books about them ever since Japanese industries nearly put Detroit automobile manufacturers out of business (and the Japanese steel industry caused similar damage to Pittsburgh). Now that Japanese computer companies and microchip makers are putting the pressure on Silicon Valley, a number of American firms have attempted to put some of the Japanese management practices into action. Unfortunately for American managers, many of the Japanese management techniques are actually Japanese communication techniques that are intertwined with the Japanese way of life or *Weltanschaaung.*

One of the communication techniques that Western managers have tried to introduce, with mixed results, is the Japanese custom of *feeling out all the people involved with an issue before making a decision.* By the time such a decision is made, all parties have subtly made their positions clear and have adjusted their stands in an effort to make them compatible with the positions taken by others. The process is more subtle than simple consensus gathering and presupposes a shared distaste for confrontation that might not transplant well in American institutions. The Japanese name for this decision-making approach is *nemawashi* (neh-mah-WAH-shee)—"root binding"—a term borrowed from the art of bonsai, in which miniature trees are created by careful pruning of limbs and roots.

The bonsai metaphor compares the way the careful pruning and repositioning of roots (people's feelings about an issue) can determine the tree's future growth (the actual decision-making and implementation of policy). The Japanese feel this approach is superior to hashing it all out in a meeting because it avoids open conflict, a social situation Japanese seek to avoid in all areas of life. For this reason, Japanese are comfortable with the nuances of indirect negotiation. In America, however, we are thoroughly committed to a system based on advocacy and confrontation: "You argue for your position, and I'll argue for mine, and may the strongest argument win." Although *nemawashi* might be difficult to transplant, it might work as an enhancement of the American management practice of "signing people up" for a proposal before it is formally argued—the practice of "getting everyone on board." The catchword for this philosophy in organizational development is "alignment"—that is, an effort to make sure all participants in a company project are pulling *with* one another, rather than *against* one another.

tirare la carretta (Italian)
To slog through the everyday dirty work. [verb]

It's Monday morning, and you are sitting at your desk, facing half a day of mindless paperwork. Or it's time for spring cleaning, and you finally have to tackle that mess in the garage. What do you say when somebody asks, in all innocence, what you are doing on this fine morning? Take a tip from the Italians, who often come up with elegant phrases for the painful necessities of life, and say you have to *tirare la carretta* (tee-RAH-ray lah cuh-REH-tuh). The literal translation of this charming phrase is "to pull the little cart." It's a good phrase to use when your partner dumps onerous and uninteresting work on you or leaves for a vacation just before the quarterly inventory. And when your children ask you why they have to do their boring old multiplication tables tonight, simply tell them that we all have to *tirare la carretta* from time to time.

gajes (Spanish)
Benefits and hazards of a job, profession, or position.
[noun]

When you get a parking place with your name on it, along
with a pay increase, that is considered a "perk" of your new
position. When you have to put up with the boss's incessant
bragging about his golf prowess, that is considered one of the
"dues you have to pay" for a promotion. The fact that you
are likely to be attacked by a hostile dog is known as an "occupational hazard" of mail delivery. And the unavoidable
responsibility for changes in the lives and livelihoods of many
people as the result of your decisions is referred to as "the
cares of office." The Spanish word *gajes* (GAH-hays) is a combination of all of the above. The literal translation is "wages,"
but in general it means *anything that you give or receive, outside the formal job description, as part of your work.* This term
admirably covers those gray areas where only your disposition and proclivities determine whether the key to the executive washroom or the privilege of being the first to arrive and
the last to leave is considered a bonus or a hardship.

plunderbund (Dutch)
Group or alliance of financial or political interests that
exploits the public. [noun]

You don't have to be a conspiracy theorist or a communist to
appreciate this descriptive word, for there isn't any doubt that
criminals and capitalists, politicos and commissars, bankers
and monopolists, guilds and cabals, have always conspired to

stop stealing from one another long enough to fleece the greater population. Whether the scam is a pyramid scheme or high-priced, shoddy products, the idea is the same: "Let's get together and take the suckers for as much as the market will bear." The next time you need a word to describe this kind of conspiracy, use *plunderbund* (PLOON-dur-boond). But don't use it in a public speech or publication unless you have the facts to back it up: Accusing people of forming *an alliance for the express purpose of defrauding the public* is probably grounds for a slander or libel suit.

Plunderbunds have a long if not entirely honorable history. Cortez and his band of freebooters formed a *plunderbund* before they departed for the shores of Mexico. Many of the companies that formed in London to trade slaves from Africa for rum in the West Indies and tobacco in America were *plunderbunds*. Nowadays, most people see parking tickets as part of municipal *plunderbunds*, while others would apply the term to certain religious television programs. Interpretations are not always unambiguous: One man's *plunderbund* is another's livelihood. But it has a good, round, condemnatory sound to it. It sounds ominous, underhanded, and despicable, which makes it an excellent candidate for a new economic pejorative.

lagniappe (French/Creole)
An unexpected gift to a stranger or customer. [noun]

To most people in the United States, this is a foreign word and a foreign concept. But to inhabitants of New Orleans, it is a part of everyday speech. The word is derived from the Creole culture, a mixture of Spanish, French, and black elements that date back to the 18th century. To this day, storekeepers and clerks keep small gifts under the counter for patient children and husbands of customers, or for people who come in and browse and don't buy anything but who have a friendly manner. A *lagniappe* (lan-YAP) is a general term for *anything extra that wasn't expected by the terms of a contract,* written or tacit. "And as a *lagniappe,* I'm going to throw in a year's worth of gas with this car," the automobile salesman might say, after the deal was signed and sealed.

If you visit a friend who has small children or plan to visit a foreign country, you might wrap a few kazoos and boxes of crayons in pretty paper and keep them handy as *lagniappes* for the children of the people you do business with or who are friendly to you. It's a custom that deserves general acceptance. It's good for business and good for the state of mind of the giver and receiver alike.

aroysgevorfeneh gelt (Yiddish)
A bad, irretrievable investment. [adjective/noun]

We have words for bonanzas and windfalls, but English doesn't have a precise word to describe *an investment that went bad and can't be retrieved.* Accountants and attorneys use technical circumlocutions, but these do not take into account the emotional anguish associated with investments that didn't turn out to be such a good idea. Yiddish, a language with many kinds of emotional nuances for various kinds of disasters, uses the adjective *aroysgevorfeneh* (ah-ROYCE-geh-vor-feneh, rhymes with "a choice orphan, eh") to describe something that is wasted or thrown away. If you feel that your words (*verter*) are unheeded, you sigh and refer to your entreaties as *aroysgevorfeneh verter*. And if your money (*gelt*) was wasted on worthless stocks or your brother-in-law's latest hot tip in the stock market or shoddy, unreturnable merchandise, then you can shake your head and declare it *aroysgevorfeneh gelt*. The phrase can also apply to wasted time that is thrown after previously wasted time. All time, however, whether it is wasted or well spent, is irretrievable.

fucha (Polish)
Using company time and resources for your own ends.
   [verb]

Unless they are self-employed, most people tend to resent their boss and/or the owners of the company that employs them. In some cases, this resentment manifests itself in a widespread, slightly rebellious form of theft. In a rigidly socialist country like Poland, where the employer and the state are one and the same, this theft can take on political connotations. This word has several related meanings, all of which are easily recognizable to workers in either capitalist or socialist economies. It can mean "moonlighting" in the simple, legitimate sense of working two or more jobs. It can also mean to do something poorly, to bungle a job. *Fucha* (FOO-hah) is most generally and colloquially used, however, to describe *the act of using company time and company resources (machines, supplies, services) to complete a job for yourself or someone else.* A metal lathe worker, for example, might use all or part of his eight hours a day to produce parts not for the factory but for his brother-in-law, who happens to be an auto mechanic.

In Poland, where the returns from guaranteed socialist employment are often supplemented by unofficial work, *fucha* is regarded as a legitimate means of meeting one's needs at the expense of an oppressive, state-controlled employer. In capitalist countries, where rapaciousness and greed appear to motivate more than one employer, the same attitude (if not the same word) is adopted by all those who use the office copier, pilfer office supplies, or work on their own projects during company time.

Many people in the West justify small-scale theft of goods and services as "fringe benefits" of their job, even if they have no grievance against their employers. A long-distance phone call here, a box of paper clips there. Perhaps if we adopted a word for it, people would realize that it is a deliberate act of rebellion or thievery, rather than just something that "everybody does." Perhaps we will even see the day when employers put up NO FUCHA! signs.

CHAPTER SIX

States of Mind

Words, Thoughts, and Beyond

Two widely divergent but interrelated experiences, psychoanalysis and work as an anthropologist, have led me to the belief that in his strivings for order, Western man has created chaos by denying that part of his self that integrates while enshrining the parts that fragment experience. These examinations of man's psyche have also convinced me that: the natural act of thinking is greatly modified by culture; Western man uses only a small fraction of his mental capabilities; there are many different and legitimate ways of thinking; we in the West value one of these ways above all others—the one we call "logic," a linear system that has been with us since Socrates.

Edward T. Hall, *Beyond Culture*

*I*s language a thought-tool, or is thought a language-tool? Are words merely vehicles by which we externalize and share our internal perceptions, or are they templates that determine how and what we think? Linguists, anthropologists, and psychologists are still debating the degree of influence language exerts on cognition, but there is little doubt that one's native tongue is a powerful formative influence on one's worldview. In the English-speaking world, people think in some ways and fail to think in other ways because of the words we do and do not have for various states of mind. Indeed, most English-speaking people equate "thinking" with "state of mind." Yet there are other languages in which there are dozens, even hundreds, of words for states of mind that do not include "thoughts" as we define them. To a certain degree, then, you can therefore begin to explore new states of mind simply by learning the right new words.

When the analyst-anthropologist Edward T. Hall states that "Western man has created chaos by denying that part of his self that integrates while enshrining the parts that fragment experience," he refers to the states of mind that we learn in our earliest schooling—and the ones that we do not learn about. The external power of Western science and technology derives from a formalization of these tendencies toward analysis (knowing about systems by breaking them into parts), reductionism (the belief that all things can be reduced to strictly physical causes), and positivism (the belief that only publicly measurable phenomena, and not the private events that take place within the minds of individuals, are worthy of study). Hall mentions the fact that we learn to use these experience-fragmenting tools but are not taught their integrative complements (that some things cannot be analyzed; that some things cannot be strictly understood as physical phenomena; that private events can and should be studied systematically).

One fundamental distinction that is built into English grammar is the difference between an *object* and a *process*. This distinction fits neatly with Newton's model of a clockwork universe. Unfortunately for those who were stuck in Newtonian thought-modes, the quantum physicists showed that the world is more like a web of inextricably interconnected processes than a series of discrete events. In the West, we are just beginning to adjust our states of mind to the worldviews uncovered by the quantum revolution. Ultimately, we will have to invent or adapt new words in order to navigate in a relativistic universe. As one of the architects of the quantum revolution, Werner Heisenberg, pointed out, "The problems of language here are really serious. We wish to speak in some way about the structure of atoms...but we cannot speak of atoms in ordinary language."

The philosopher Alan Watts made the same point in *The Way of Zen*, speaking as a metaphysician rather than as a physicist. But he agreed with Heisenberg that the disparity between our customary mental categories and the model of the world that has been uncovered by modern physics is a problem of language:

> Thus the task of education is to make children fit to live in a society by persuading them to learn and accept its codes—the rules and conventions of communication whereby the society holds itself together. There is first the spoken language. The child is taught to accept "tree" and not "boojum" as the agreed sign for *that* (pointing to the object). We have no difficulty in understanding that the word *tree* is a matter of convention. What is much less obvious is that convention also governs the delineation of the thing to which the word is assigned. For the child has to be taught not only what words are to stand for what things, but also the way in which his culture has tacitly agreed to divide things from each other, to mark out the boundaries within our daily experience. Thus scientific convention decides whether an eel shall be a fish or a snake, and grammatical convention determines what experiences shall be called objects and what shall be called events or actions. How arbitrary such conventions may be can be seen from the question "What

happens to my fist [noun-object] when I open my hand?" The object miraculously vanishes because an action was disguised by a part of speech usually assigned to a thing! In English the differences between things and actions are clearly, if not always logically, distinguished, but a great number of Chinese words do duty for both nouns and verbs—so that one who thinks in Chinese has little difficulty in seeing that objects are also events, that our world is a collection of processes rather than entities.

Can we learn to think in new categories, or even to use our minds in ways that do not involve thinking? Let us perform what the Germans call *Gedankenexperiment*, a "thought-experiment." Read the words and their definitions in this chapter. See if you can recognize an experiential reverberation (*yoin*) or a state of emotional and spiritual revitalization (*sabsung*) when you run across one of them in your life. Think about *ta* and *wen* and see if you don't understand life and thought in a different way. Meditate on *mu* and watch your mind struggling with thoughts that can't be captured in nets made of words. See if you can find a way to use these words and others from the Arabic, Balinese, Indonesian, Italian, Japanese, Korean, Navajo, Sanskrit, and Spanish lexicons in your life, work, or thought. Observe yourself. And see if you don't start experiencing the inner and outer worlds in new ways.

sabsung (Thai)
To slake an emotional or spiritual thirst, to be revitalized.
[verb]

Have you ever returned home from a stressful and exhausting business trip, listened to some favorite music, and felt a sense of psychic and spiritual revitalization, as if the music had poured extra life into your soul? Have you experienced a strangely similar sensation in a very different context, where a few precious words from a special person seemed to soak into your being the way rain soaks into the parched ground after a drought? The Thai word *sabsung* (SOB-soong) serves to describe both kinds of revitalizing experiences, *a slaking of both the mind's and the heart's thirst.* Have you ever felt that something is wrong in your life, but you can't quite state what it is? Recognizing that one has certain spiritual and psychological needs is something that can make life richer. *Sabsung* is both the act of quenching metaphysical thirsts and the feeling that comes with the fulfillment of these hard-to-define but all-important needs.

The literal meaning of *sabsung* refers to the physical act of immersing in liquid something that has become dry. But the personal connotation points to a kind of spiritual emotion, a specific reaction that comes from one's soul in response to the slaking "substance," whether it is literally a drink of water, a kind word, or a beautiful work of art. You can use the word for special moments when you encounter a great painting, or else see your family after a painful separation, or reread a favorite poem. You can also do yourself a favor by seeking or demanding it when the stresses and complications of the world threaten to overwhelm you: "I badly need to *sabsung.* I'm retiring to my room with the *Rubaiyat,* a jug of wine, and my collection of heavy-metal records."

yoin (Japanese)
Experiential reverberation that continues to move you long after the initial external stimulus has ceased. [noun]

The literal definition of this word refers to the reverberations that continue for a long time after a well-cast bell is struck, but the more interesting colloquial definition refers to a bell that is made of human feelings rather than metal. Have you ever felt a pang of pure, sweet sadness when you heard a song on the radio that reminded you of your youth and then you realized that you might someday look back upon *this* moment in the same way? Does a certain poem or a sculpture touch something deep inside your heart? Has a painting ever leapt from the eyes and hands of a painter, or a character jumped from the mind of a playwright, instantaneously traversed the centuries, and rang your emotions like a bell?

Yoin (yoh-EEN) is the Japanese word for *any kind of moving experience that causes profound emotional reverberations.* In Japan, the act of looking out a window at the garden, the moon, or the countryside is considered to be an aesthetic and emotional act, much like the experience of viewing a work of art; therefore, *yoin* can be applied to the feeling that wells up when one drinks sake while looking at the freshly fallen snow, or when one takes a sharp breath at the sight of the moon through a blossoming cherry tree.

Nostalgia is the English word for an experience that is somewhat less profound, for nostalgia evokes the feeling of a fond remembrance and a bittersweet yearning for old times. *Yoin* is closer to a re-experiencing of an eternal moment, which is triggered by a memory but exists in the present as well as the past. *Yoin* is an existential act of resonance with something that *is*, not an active task of recapturing something that was.

kut (Korean)
Spiritual trance performance. [noun]

Ninety percent of the medical treatment in the world is performed by native healers, many of whom accomplish their diagnosis or treatment or both while in a state of induced trance. In more than a few hunting-gathering cultures, the entranced healer, known as a *shaman*, temporarily adopts the personalities of various gods and spirits in a phenomenon known to anthropologists as "spirit possession." In Korea, the shamanic ritual for healing is triggered by drumming, dancing, and chanting, as it is in other shamanic cultures, inducing a form of spirit possession in a shaman, usually a woman, known as a *mudang*, whose consciousness is then inhabited by a series of spirits, one after another.

The distinguishing characteristic of *kut* (KOOT), the Korean variation of shamanic healing trance, is the mudang's *act of donning and shedding different pieces of clothing as the different spirits take over*. In some cultures, shamanism is restricted to the jurisdiction of a few specialists—as it is in Western medical practice. In other cultures, such as the Korean, voluntary spirit possession is widespread. There is a definite need for this word in our society to describe that state of mind experienced by people of all ages (although it used to be confined to the young) and both genders (although it used to be an exclusively female phenomenon) when they seek to heal themselves of disappointment in love or career by "shopping"—a ritual that often involves trying on a variety of different pieces of clothing while in a trancelike state. A similar ritual is associated with teenagers of both genders when they try out various outfits before going on a date. If this word were to be adopted for English usage, one might say: "You should have seen Judy in Macy's—she was in a state of *kut*!"

ta (Chinese)
To understand things and thus take them lightly. [verb]

Westerners don't have a monopoly on the ethic of "work hard, get ahead, and leave the meaning of it all to the ministers and professors." Every scripture of every major religion has a parable about the pitfalls of mistaking the price of something for its value. Ambition and moral blinders are a pancultural trait. The Chinese language contains a word that bespeaks a value and attitude toward understanding that might serve well in *any* language: *ta*, for *a kind of understanding of a situation that enables a person to take the situation lightly*. A person who takes anything too seriously or is too heavily involved in business affairs is said to be *puta* ("not *ta*"). Lin Yutang included *ta* in the appendix of *The Importance of Living* as one of the Chinese words he found "extremely difficult to render into English."

One can *ta* office politics or domestic life, a personal

tragedy or a difficult physical or mental task. One can *ta* "the human heart" or "the ways of the world" (see *tao* in chapter eight). One can also *ta* the whole shebang: *Takuan* means "to have seen through life," a state of mind that enables humans to live in a world dominated by unfettered ambition and to put up with temporary disadvantages or obscurity or poverty. In this sense, *takuan* is an understanding that the world works in strange and sometimes unfair ways, an understanding that things sometimes can't be understood.

In contemporary terms, one might imagine someone saying, "I had a hard time dealing with the fact that the overbearing guy at the next desk was promoted—until I got some *ta* about it." "He or she has great *ta*" could become a great compliment to bestow on a person who tends to be savvy, understanding, and sympathetic. Or, when the moral pendulum swings away from preoccupation with material wealth, the sage businessperson of the future might say, "I made $10,000 less than I would have made otherwise, but I went out of my way to get some deep *ta* out of the deal."

Gedankenexperiment (German)
Thought-experiment. [noun]

Certain thoughts are so potent that they change the course of human events. In religion, these thoughts are spiritual in nature. In the arts, they are called "inspiration." Even in the sciences, the experience of seminal thoughts by key people has shaped scientific history. Newton and the image of a falling apple is a classic example: The realization that the fall of an apple and the orbits of the stars are governed by the same law led to the laws of motion and gravitation. Einstein's theory of relativity was another scientific milestone that was triggered by and explained via a series of *Gedankenexperiments* (gay-DAWN-ken-exper-ee-ments)—literally, "thought-experiments." It isn't necessary to grind up the world and put it in a test tube in order to experiment; in some matters, all you need to do is *think* about a problem in the right way.

Einstein, who was a notoriously uninspired student, grew fascinated with a personal *Gedankenexperiment* when he was young: What would he see, the young Einstein wondered, if he could ride on a light beam and look at himself in a mirror? If he was traveling as fast as light could travel, his reflection would never reach the mirror—so what would he see? This physics experiment, which could never be performed except in the form of a thought, kept drawing the young man's attention (while he was failing his classes in school). When an older Einstein solved the problem posed by this curious mental image, he overturned traditional scientific notions about space and time.

Some psychologists say that all humans perform *Gedankenexperiments*, and that the ability to guess tomorrow's weather, predict the course of the stock market, figure out what a chess opponent is likely to do is the aspect of consciousness that sets us apart from animals—the ability to simulate the future and to fit the simulation into a scenario that makes sense and explains other phenomena observed in the past. The kind of word problems you find in mathematics class are a variety of *Gedankenexperiments*, especially if they force you to think about something in a new way. Consider a thought-experiment from the field of probability theory, widely known as the "Ehrenfest problem": Suppose you are a prisoner who has been condemned to die, but the king decides to give you a break. He gives you two white stones and two black stones and two identical urns. You can put the stones in the urns in any combination you wish. The king will shuffle the urns, then you select one ball from one of the urns. Pick a white stone and you live. How can you optimize your odds?

The answer to the Ehrenfest problem is a model for how to think about similar problems related to probability. If you put one white stone in one urn and the other white stone along with both black stones in the other urn, your odds will be increased from the 50–50 odds expected from chance: If you choose the urn with the white stone, you are certain to live. If you choose the other urn, your chances of drawing the white stone are one in three. The odds of drawing either urn are one in two. Multiply ½ times certainty (1.0) and add that to ½ multiplied by ⅓, and you get odds of two in three that you will win. The same formula works more impressively for larger numbers: If you have 100 white stones and 100 black stones, put one white stone in one urn all by itself and combine the other 99 white stones with all 100 black stones in the other urn.

The next time somebody asks, "What would happen if . . ." a good reply might be, "Why don't we perform a *Gedankenexperiment* and see how it turns out? Suppose I have two urns and two hundred stones . . ."

Weltschmerz (**German**)
**A gloomy, romanticized world-weary sadness, experienced
    most often by privileged youth. [noun]**

In the 1980s, a series of shocking acts of self-destruction by
young Americans, part of an inexplicable epidemic of
teenage suicides, has led to a series of court cases to determine whether the lyrics of certain nihilistic "heavy metal"
rock-music groups could be held responsible for these
statements of ultimate despair. Although the courts have
upheld the First Amendment rights of musical composers to
publish lyrics without taking legal responsibility for actions
that might be taken by disturbed individuals who might
hear the songs, American parents continue to be disturbed
by the evidence of a death-loving romanticism at the heart
of the richest civilization in history.

Today's parents may take some comfort from knowing that
this phenomenon is nothing new. In the 1930s, Billie Holli-
day's recording of "Gloomy Sunday" also set off an epidemic
of suicides. And in the 18th century, the great German poet
Goethe gave us *The Sorrows of Young Werther*, about an aesthetically minded youth who was simply too sensitive to live. It
seems that every generation dabbles with *the idea that languid
sorrow and ultimate self-destruction is romantic* in some way.

Weltschmerz (literally "world-grief," pronounced VELT-
shmairtz) is the name the Germans gave to this state of
mind. Although Werther was the paradigm example, he was
part of a whole literary tradition in Europe: The French pre-
Romantic Chateaubriand wrote *Atala* and *René*, two classic

Weltschmerz tales; the sickly, despondent Italian poet Leopardi and the British Lord Byron also wrote about sensitive, eccentric youths, often misunderstood geniuses, who fail to adapt themselves to the cruel realities of the world.

The literary characters who suffer from *Weltschmerz*, despite their differences in nationality, seem to share one key attribute: They are often the sons (less often, the daughters) of rich people, who do not need to worry about hunger or a roof over their heads and so are free to indulge themselves languidly in feeling sorrow for their existential state. *Weltschmerz*, in other words, is often a disease of the healthy and wealthy.

conmoción (Spanish)
Emotion held in common by a group or gathering. [noun]

Whenever a nation weeps in commemoration of slain heroes or the population of a sports stadium rises up and shouts with one voice, or whenever the funeral of a political martyr erupts in a riot, the people who participate in the event experience a rare and often frightening variety of human emotion—the kind of deep emotion that can be held in common, temporarily, by a gathering of people who may be strangers to one another. The Spanish-speaking people reserve the word *conmoción* (cone-moe-see-OWN) for this kind of group emotion. The word is deliberately not restricted to events that get out of hand. A more precise Spanish equivalent for "commotion" would be *jaleo*, and the Spanish word for riot is *motín*.

The way in which abstractions can cause people to cluster into social groups is one of the distinct characteristics of the human species. All other organisms group according to urgings of their genes, but a group of humans who do not know or care for one another can be welded into a cohesive group by hearing the right words. Whether the wielder of the words is a demagogue or a prophet, a healer or a rabble-rouser, any person who seeks to rouse a crowd to action must first incite them to a feeling of *conmoción.* It is a word that can be used in politics, sports, and even entertainment: The different kinds of crowds to be found at a political rally, a football game, or a concert are similarly susceptible to the arousal of *conmoción,* for they have, by their presence, declared themselves to be in sympathy with one another about the aims of that political party, the importance of football, or the beauty of that music, and tacitly declare a temporary truce regarding other cultural differences. With the urban population density increasing steadily, *conmoción* is a word to keep handy: *the sometimes dangerous, always thrilling feeling of emotional resonance with a large crowd.*

Bettschwere (German)
A state of consciousness too ponderous for anything but sleep. [noun]

Have you ever awakened on a day off, remembered that you had made plans to get out and enjoy yourself, but ended up just gazing out the window at the bright, clear, inviting day before turning over and going back to sleep, breathing a guiltless sigh in your delicious torpor? This peculiarly decadent frame of mind is not the kind of exhaustion that comes from hard work or lack of sleep. It is simply, as the Germans say, a state of "bed heaviness"—*Bettschwere* (BET-shvare-eh)—in which you realize that you are *temporarily feeling too heavy to perform anything as mentally and physically demanding as getting out of bed.*

If somebody tries to arouse you and you don't really feel like getting up and joining the fully conscious members of your family or community in merriment or livelihood, just tell them you are in a state of *Bettschwere*. And while they are wondering what the heck you mean, you can grab a few more precious minutes of slumber.

palatyi (**Bantu**)
A mythical monster that scratches at the door. [noun]

It's one thing for things to go bump in the night. It's another matter when they start—or you think they start—scratching at your door. What could possibly be more frightening, especially to those who live in the back country, than the belief that *a large, strange, clawed creature is scratching at your door on a cold night*—when you don't have a dog or cat? The Bantu-speaking people of Africa know all about this beast, who they call *palatyi*. And descendants of West African Bantu-speaking slaves still speak of a malevolent supernatural being thought to haunt the Georgetown area of South Carolina, an animal-like, door-scratching ghost called the *plat-eye*, or *plat-eye prowl*.

Whenever the hour is late and the talk turns to scary stories, you might mention this folk tradition that survived the harrowing middle passage and the dark centuries of slavery. Is the night-scratching *plat-eye* a figment of folk superstition? A variation on a theme from the collective unconscious? Or do those folks in West Africa and South Carolina have particular experience with a kind of beast that is best left unanswered when it comes to call? It's easy enough to test the hypotheses—if you ever hear a scratching at your door, late at night, and the hairs on the back of your head start to organize themselves into strict rows, why don't you simply get up and open the door?

maya (Sanskrit)
The mistaken belief that a symbol is the same as the reality it represents. [noun]

The word *maya* is related to the English word *measure*, because the root *ma* means "to measure or lay out," as in laying out the plan of a building. It can be defined as "the creation of forms." All the countless insects, goddesses, demons, and wise men are part of it, as are all the empires and planets and cycles of history. Those who know that the goal of Hindu theology is to achieve liberation from the bonds of illusion often mistake *maya* for a strictly negative label denoting the illusions that cause suffering. But this is also an illusion, for the deeper meaning of the term is "existence." *Maya* relates not only to the endless play of forms and the void from which they spring, but to *the dangerous attach-*

ments people tend to develop in relation to their conceptual maps of the world. The founder of general semantics, Alfred Korzybski, called this tendency to believe that one's measurements are also the very things being measured "the illusion of mistaking the map for the territory."

An ancient Hindu myth tells of a semidivine ascetic, Narada, who was granted a boon by the god Vishnu and who asked to be shown the secret of *maya.* Vishnu, after warning the seeker not to inquire into this ultimate secret, told Narada to dive into a nearby lake. Narada emerged from the water as Sushila, the daughter of the great king. In due course, she married an ambitious king who fought many battles and conquered a great empire. Sushila led an exciting life in her various palaces and bore many children who in turn bore her grandchildren. Toward the end of her life, however, a terrible dispute broke out between her husband and father, and they embarked on a bloody war that took the lives of Sushila's husband, her father, her sons, and her grandsons. With a heart-weariness that no mortal had ever known, she piled the bodies of her loved ones onto a great pyre, ignited it, then dived into the flames. She emerged from the lake that Vishnu had pointed out so many years before, dripping wet, transformed back to Narada, a male ascetic.

"Who is this son whose death you are bewailing?" asked Vishnu, leading Narada out of the crystal pool of *maya.* What Narada experienced, the god explained, was the surface of *maya.* Not even the gods know its depths. Reality, by its nature, is never what it seems, just as a word is not the object it symbolizes and a map is not the territory it describes. Sentient beings must not lose sight of the void when they perceive the world as form, because to see the world as void is to lose attachment to the world of forms. *Maya* is a word that is ripe for adaptation here and now. The next time you see somebody in despair because of her cash-flow situation, love life, or even the state of the world, you can remind her of *maya*, of Narada's grief, and ask them, "Who is this *you* are bewailing?"

Feierabend (German)
Festive frame of mind at the end of the working day.
[noun]

Here we say "Thank God it's Friday" at the end of the work-week, but that doesn't cover *the feeling of warm, relaxed, comfortable euphoria that can accompany the end of the working day.* In Germany, the men simply say "*Feierabend*" (fire-AH-bend), and that's that: Work is over and the fun begins. *Feier* means "celebration" and *Abend* means "evening." Celebration-evening? Right. *Feierabend* is that time of the day when all deeds are done; when the clock strikes and the factory closes; when you go home or to the pub; when you put up your feet and have the dog bring your slippers.

As you might guess, *Feierabend* is—or was—for menfolk only. Women have no *Feierabend*. But since we are importing the word, we might as well modify it for the modern environment, where women are just as happy to leave their factories and offices and head home. *Feierabend* is more a state of mind than a word; it's the time of day that's worth living for; the time of day to celebrate. In Germany, *Feierabend* is so popular that it has long been used as a greeting. *"Feierabend!"* can be heard all over the land as men tip their hats, go home to the wife, have a beer, have supper. In this era of two-career households and rampant workaholism, we all need to remind ourselves that it's beneficial, approved, and fun to stop working and relax: "Honey, I'm home, and I'm full of *Feierabend!*"

cuor contento (**Italian**)
The way a happy, even-tempered person feels. [noun]

There are words for strange states of mind, ugly states of mind, painful states of mind, deluded or enlightened states of mind. Here is a word to apply to the mental and emotional state of those rare individuals who don't seem to fret, don't seem to fly off the handle, aren't necessarily benighted or enlightened, and don't seem to carry the weight of the world on their shoulders. The Italians call such a person a *cuor contento*—literally, a "happy heart." (In America, you might say that the ubiquitous "happy face" is the symbol of this kind of unconditional cheeriness.) Some people say you have to be born with the right disposition. Others say you have to be born to rich parents. Psychoanalysts and evangelists say you can achieve such a state, even if it isn't one of your natural attributes, through work or faith. In any case, when the fellow at the next desk or the woman in the car pool seems to beam along, even in the face of difficulties, you can mention that it is good to see a *cuor contento* once in a while.

zanshin (Japanese)
A state of relaxed mental alertness in the face of danger.
[noun]

The fabled martial arts of Japan, from *karate* (literally, "empty-handed combat") to the kind of swordmanship portrayed in samurai films, have been glorified and mythologized by books and movies. The rigors of the physical training necessary to become a martial artist are well known. And the element of a profound mental discipline has also been popularized, if not always well understood, in the West. In fact, if you were to ask a master martial artist what his or her most important weapon might be, the answer received would undoubtedly be more along the lines of a state of mind rather than a secret fighting technique. If you ever watch a karate match or see a reasonably authentic samurai film, you have witnessed the exhibition of this most important mental component (or at least an external facsimile of it), known as *zanshin* (zon-SHEEN).

Many karate matches, and almost all sword battles, begin with both opponents poised in *a state of relaxed alertness.* This is in extreme contrast to the Western mental component of combat, as in boxing, where both opponents seem to be psyching themselves up into a frenzy, hopping and jogging in place, seemingly unable to contain their energy. In true sword battles, however, the combatant who betrays this kind of nervous energy is usually the one who finds his head or other limbs rolling on the ground a moment later. As any aikido master can demonstrate, a tensed muscle is unable to react as swiftly and surely as a relaxed muscle.

Zanshin is not easy to attain. Many years of mental and physical discipline are required before a martial artist can face an opponent without anxiety or tension. In a profound sense, the martial artist must learn to set aside that part of himself that cares about winning or losing, fear or bravery. The perfectly trained warrior faces his opponent, adopts a relaxed posture, and concentrates on his own energy center, the *hara* or *tanden* in the center of his body. The first opponent to break concentration is the one who loses.

We no longer face the prospect of hand-to-hand combat on the streets, except when we find ourselves in the wrong neighborhood at the wrong time of day. But to many, business is warfare, and there are many instances when we must face opponents in boardrooms or courtrooms. In those instances, the breathing, meditation, and physical exercises that lead to the mental state of *zanshin* can make the difference between victory and defeat. Remember the look on Perry Mason's face when he turned to face the D.A., after the prosecution had presented an airtight case against Perry's client? That's a kind of *zanshin*. Simply reminding yourself that such a state of mind exists, and that you can attain it by calming your emotions and focusing your attention, can carry you a long way toward your goal.

nadi (Balinese)
To temporarily inhabit another dimension. [verb]

Trance is a word with a bad reputation in Western culture, and it doesn't have terribly salutary connotations in many Eastern religions either. Here we associate it with a state of stupor or hypnotic enslavement, of total dissolution of will (look at a family that's been watching television for a few hours to get a picture of this kind of trance). Hindus and Buddhists regard our normal perceptions of the world to be a kind of trance, a belief-system hypnosis that enthralls us to illusion and thus enslaves us to suffering. Curiously, despite the bad reputation this state of consciousness seems to have gained worldwide, many artistic and scientific creations have been conceived while their creators were in such a trance state. Great artists such as Mozart and Robert Louis Stevenson and Nobel Prize–winning scientists have admitted that some of their greatest works emerged from a kind of trance state. Many of the observed cases of "lightning calculators" who have demonstrated mathematical abilities far beyond the normal seem to perform their mental feats in a trance. Is it possible that there is *a beneficial variety of trance*, as well as a harmful one? Is it possible that some people simply know how to step into an alternate dimension of consciousness for a short time, and then return bearing gifts?

Consider the mental state the Balinese call *nadi* (NOD-ee): It is derived from the Balinese *dadi*, which means "to become." In Bali, it is not confined to the stupefied or the mentally ill, but is part of their art and religion. During a performance of one of their renowned shadow plays, for example, dozens of Balinese spectators fall into violent trances in which they seize swords and act as if they were inhabitants of the mythical realm depicted by the performance! To the Balinese, the entranced ones are not deluded; they have simply become temporary inhabitants of another dimension. Judging from the beauty and harmony of Balinese life, this temporary derangement doesn't seem to do any individual or social damage; to the contrary, some observers have suggested that *nadi* is one of the means by which the inhabitants of this island have achieved the tranquil and aesthetic culture for which they are renowned.

In Western terms, every member of the audience at a film or play "willingly suspends disbelief" when the house lights darken and the curtain goes up. We pretend that Errol Flynn is Robin Hood and forget that he is an actor, and a deceased one at that. *Nadi* takes suspension of disbelief one or more steps further into the realm where the audience members actually participate in the eternal drama that is symbolized by the temporal performance on stage. Certain everyday-life circumstances might call for this term as well: Whenever you scream during a horror movie, use body language while watching a wrestling match, or partake in the hushed concentration of a grandstand full of home-team fans, you are in the presence of a variety of *nadi*. If you know a thinker or an artist or an "absentminded professor" who seems to be "in another world" part of the time, don't insult or disturb the entranced one: He or she may simply be in *nadi*.

hart ducha **(Polish)**
Self-mastery in the face of internal and external forces.
    [noun]

Many spiritual and psychological traditions, from Native American rituals to Eastern disciplines, emphasize the kind of stoic, disciplined state of mind necessary for self-mastery. In Poland, a nation where the fate of the citizens and particularly the peasantry has often been in the hands of the feudal ruling classes or of foreign invaders, the concept of individual dignity in the face of attempted humiliation has been joined to the notion of psychological and physiological self-mastery. A man (it is considered to be primarily a male trait) who has *hart ducha* (heart DOO-ha) is not only one who has gained control of his desires and appetites and therefore subjected his body to his mind and spirit, but *one who does not cry out, cower, flee, surrender, or compromise* in the face of attacks on his rights or independence.

So strong is the tradition of disciplined independence that even feudal lords were required to inquire politely before they were permitted to enter the hut of a poor peasant. More recently, the Solidarity movement, and its most well known hero, Lech Walesa, epitomized *hart ducha* (literally, "hard spirit") in the face of opposition by the military rulers of Poland. It is a term of honor and should not be applied lightly, but certainly ought to be applied to those men and women of our present era and Western culture who exhibit simple dignity and self-control while performing the most menial tasks. These people are all around us, if we take the time to notice them. New immigrants to America, for example, who may have held positions of power and respect in their native lands before they escaped political oppression and who now work as laborers and servants at day, study English at night, and maintain their dignity in the midst of greatly reduced circumstances, are among those who have earned this honor. *Hart ducha* is displayed by the Russian surgeon who drives a cab in Manhattan and the Vietnamese engineer who works in a laundry in L.A.

Katzenjammer (German)
Monumentally severe hangover. [noun]

The pleasant state of intoxication that can be produced by the consumption of alcoholic beverages is a favorite state of mind, at least part of the time, of at least part of the population of virtually every culture on the planet. And the unpleasant feelings of nausea, headache, and nervous hypersensitivity that can occur the morning after a night of festive imbibing is similarly despised by every alcohol-loving culture. In the West, we call these unpleasant aftereffects a hangover. In Germany, the fun-loving students of the 19th century came up with a term for a very severe case of this, the kind where even the softest sounds have the impact of unearthly shrieking. The word *Katzenjammer* (KOTZ-uhn-yomur) is familiar to Americans because of the early comic strip "The Katzenjammer Kids," but few Americans realize that the word has dual meanings in German: The literal meaning refers to the sounds that cats make when they are engaging in the procreative act; the informal meaning refers to *a hangover of terminal severity.*

Perhaps the Germans actually suffer, on average, from more severe hangovers than we do here in the United States. Why else would they eat green herring as a cure? We can adopt this word for general social benefit and as a means of possibly saving our friends from the consequences of their revelry. Next New Year's Eve, take a look around and see if there isn't at least one person to whom you can say, "One more of those drinks, my friend, and you'll be setting yourself up for a real *Katzenjammer.*"

Schadenfreude (German)
Joy that one feels as a result of someone else's misfortune. [noun]

Why do people laugh at cartoons that show people slipping on banana peels? What is so funny about the way the Three Stooges bonk one another? One of the peculiar defining characteristics of the human race seems to be related to our strange and sometimes sadistic sense of humor. *Schadenfreude* (SHOD-en-froyd-eh) is the German word for the kind of *joy or laughter that is evoked by witnessing somebody else's pain or bad luck.* It is one of those traits that sets us apart from animals, but nobody has come up with a plausible reason for explaining why we do it. Although it is possible that the sight of another chimpanzee (particularly a rival) in distress can be a pleasurable experience even to nonhuman primates, it takes a true human being to think there is anything *funny* about it. This trait is found among Americans and Brazilians, Manhattanites and Hottentots, and it isn't even confined to adults: Any clown could tell you that the pratfall is the royal road to a toddler's funny bone.

Since this word strikes deep into the mysterious heart of the human condition, nobody is quite sure what the idea really means: Because it names the phenomenon but does not explain it, *Schadenfreude* can be all-purpose, tailored to your feelings at the time you see an opportunity to use it. The next time somebody trips and spills his popcorn, prompting your companion to burst into laughter and then look at you guiltily, you can choose a world-weary but essentially sympathetic expression and say, with a warmth tinged by sadness, "Ah. *Schadenfreude*." Or you can look condescending and coldly say, "Ah. *Schadenfreude*." Unless, of course, you choose neutrality and shrug your shoulders, adopt a puzzled facial expression, and mutter, in a baffled tone, "Ah. *Schadenfreude*."

mu (Japanese)
No-thing, no-mind. [noun]

To those who do not understand it, the Zen tradition can seem more like a Japanese version of vaudeville than a serious religion. This impression comes from the sometimes illogical, sometimes humorous questions and answers known as *koans*, which help to define the practice by illustrating the interactions between students and masters. Perhaps the most well known *koan* is "What is the sound of one hand clapping?" Like a joke, which loses much of its flavor when it is explained, this *koan* is truly untranslatable, even into words of the native language. The answer is not meant to be a set of words but a state of mind. Less famous but perhaps even more quintessentially Zen is the *koan* and its answer that has come to be known as "Joshu's *mu*."

"Does the dog have the Buddha nature?" asked a student of Joshu's. To which Joshu replied, *"Mu!"* The word *mu* (MOO) is variously translated as "not" or "no-thing," and in this context, if it can be explained at all in words, the meaning is not that dogs lack the Buddha nature, but that the very question itself indicates that the student is wrong-fully thinking in terms of distinctions. And when a Zen student becomes enlightened, all such distinctions disappear. Which is why Joshu once answered *"Mu!"* when he was asked if he meant that the dog did *not* have the Buddha nature. *Mu* in this context means *not what you are thinking*!

This word can come in handy in those rare but important times when somebody is asking you a question that cannot be answered because the person is barking up the wrong tree, thinking in the wrong terms, looking in the wrong place. Just make your eyes very wide, compose your features into an authoritative expression, and shout *"Mu!"* Perhaps, like Joshu, you will startle them into an entirely different state of mind!

buddhi (Sanskrit)
Intuitive direct knowledge. [noun]

What kind of knowledge do you gain when you awaken from a dream? What do you know when you know that you are awake? This is a slippery kind of knowledge if you define knowledge in the sense of testable, verifiable truths that Western science and scholarship accept. Knowledge is only partially a matter of facts and demonstrations. Ultimately, it is a state of mind. You can perform tests in dreams and remain convinced that you are awake. But when you truly awaken from a dream (or, as Buddha did, from the dream that is life, also known as *maya*), you know something directly and so deeply that it is a state of being. In this sense, it refers to a kind of knowledge that is intuitive, that stems from the internal senses as well as from those we use for external observation.

The experience of *buddhi*, or *direct intuitive knowledge*, is one that everybody has every day. (The word comes from the same root as *Buddha*, which means "the awakened one." The syllables are stressed as in the word *buddy*, but *buddhi* is pronounced to rhyme with "stood he.") We simply don't talk about it that much in our external, pragmatic, rationalistic culture. Apollo astronaut Edgar Mitchell, however, who was a paradigmatic example of the very pinnacle of pragmatic, empirical training, and whose life depended on the validity of scientific principles and technological knowledge, experienced a kind of *buddhi* regarding the entire planet Earth as he floated in space during a spacewalk on his return from the moon. He used the Greek-derived word *noetic* rather than the Sanskrit *buddhi*, but the experience he described was identical:

> The first thing that came to mind as I looked at Earth was its incredible beauty. Even the spectacular photographs do not do

it justice. It was a majestic sight—a splendid blue-and-white jewel suspended against a velvet black sky. How peacefully, how harmoniously, how marvelously it seemed to fit into the evolutionary pattern by which the universe is maintained. In a peak experience, the presence of divinity became almost palpable and I *knew* that life in the universe was not just an accident based on random processes. This knowledge came to me directly—noetically. It was not a matter of discursive reasoning or logical abstraction. It was an experiential cognition. It was knowledge gained through private subjective awareness, but it was—and still is—every bit as real as the objective data upon which, say, the navigational program or the communications system were based.

Buddhi is something that everyone uses every day, although most people don't pay enough attention to it to wonder whether it has a name or whether it can be trained like our other mental faculties. How do you know you are in love? Who is the person that goes away when you are asleep? Why can't we explain "greenness" to congenitally blind people? There will be times in your life, and they might be crucially important times, when you will know something with great internal certainty, yet you will be unable to explain how you know it. When you are stuck in this dilemma, say with sincerity that your knowledge is as direct as it is difficult to explain: "You know, *buddhi* certainty." If you put your feelings into your words, the person you are trying to convince will apprehend what you are trying to say—through *buddhi*, of course.

CHAPTER SEVEN

Life Is But a Dream

The Jargon of Mental Technologists

Western man sees his system of logic as synonymous with the truth. For him it is the only road to reality. Yet Freud educated us to the complexities of the psyche, helping his readers to look at dreams as a legitimate mental process that exists quite apart from the linearity of manifest thought. But his ideas were from the outset strenuously resisted, particularly by scientists and engineers, who were still wedded to a Newtonian model. When taken seriously, Freudian thinking shook the very foundations of conventional thought. Freud's followers, particularly Fromm and Jung, undeterred by popular stereotypes and the tremendous prestige of the physical sciences, added to his theories and bridged the gap between the linear world of logic and the integrative world of dreams.

Edward T. Hall, *Beyond Culture*

$\mathcal{D}$reaming is a realm in which we have a great deal to learn from the non-Western world. Although Western science and technology have produced superb methods for predicting and controlling the external environments, we are still amateurs in the realms of interior technology. We 20th-century Americans all learn how to turn on televisions, ride elevators, and open pop-top cans, but nobody teaches us how to dream. We spend a third of our lives in another dimension. You would think more people would want to know what they do in that nightly other world. We have extensive vocabularies for describing the functions and malfunctions of automobiles and airplanes, lawn mowers and toasters, but we don't have very many words for the ways in which we can predict, control, and learn from our mental lives, especially that part of it that continues when we sleep.

Tracing the arcane course of oneirology (dream study) is like trying to solve a constantly shifting crossword puzzle. Oneirology is an older art than you might think. Joseph and Daniel, two of the more prominent Old Testament dream workers, learned their craft from practitioners of traditions that were already ancient when biblical events occurred. All the world's great religions use scriptures that either mention dreams prominently or, like the Moslem Koran, were actually written in dreams. The most significant clues to effective dream-work techniques are scattered among unlikely sources, hidden away on dusty shelves in books on mythology, theology, history, anthropology, and the occult.

Dream researchers have ascertained that all human beings dream an average of one and one-half hours every night. Over the course of an average lifetime, each of us spends about four years in that other dimension. Because few people in industrial Western culture understand its language, most of our entire civilization has fallen into the trap of assuming that nothing useful happens in that other world. To those diligent or talented dream farers who have unlocked its secrets, however, the dreamworld is a gateway to knowledge and power. The reason we forget, the moment we open our eyes, the lessons we receive from these inner institutes of enlightenment is deceptively simple: We forget our dreams because nobody taught us how to remember, and because our waking consciousness depends upon a kind of selective inattention to interior senses. There are many time-tested ways for retraining the inner attention processes; the knowledge has existed for thousands of years, but it is only now beginning to emerge from obscurity. In part, this reemergence of ancient knowledge will cause an expansion of our vocabularies.

When I started looking for untranslatable words, a surprising proportion of dream-related words came to my attention. I found that a rich tradition of dream lore had long existed in many places and in many eras—from the dream-working tribes of Malaya and the dream lamaseries of the Himalayas to the dream shamans of the Iroquois. Taoist philosophers foreshadowed the findings of Gestalt psychologists centuries in advance. Thousands of years before Freud and Jung debated their theories of dream interpretation, sophisticated dream-work systems thrived in every quarter of the world.

In the West, only a few relatively wealthy souls engage in dream exploration, with the help of specialists known as psychotherapists. In some parts of Malaysia, however, every person in the poorest Senoi village has access to dream wisdom, via the dream-work specialists known as *halaks*. In America we think the waking world is the only reality, but certain Arabic speaking experts know of the *alam al-mithral*. We have a word for nightmares, but the Bantu-speaking tribes of Africa know about *bilita mpatshi*. These words, along with others from Australia, France, Indonesia, and Mexico, reveal the depth of the inner world that hitherto has been uncharted in the West.

Even if it is only remotely possible, the potential rewards of being in contact with our dreams seems well worth pursuing. Sensual pleasure, practical knowledge, creative inspiration, inner wisdom, emotional tranquillity, extrasensory perception, or even a hot tip for the seventh race at Belmont—whatever the quest, the answer may be waiting for you just beyond the borders of consciousness. The first step in learning a new discipline is to learn its lexicon. In this sense, learning new words about dreams and dream work can lead directly to changes in your mental life. Now that you know you can have *bilita mpatshi* as well as nightmares, perhaps your unconscious image-processor will begin sending more blissful dreams your way, and perhaps your own inner helpers will come to your aid to furnish guidance that you can find from no other source.

halak (Indonesian/non-Kamian)
Dream guide. [noun]

"As a member of a scientific expedition travelling through the unexplored equatorial rain forest of the Central Range of the Malay Peninsula in 1935, I was introduced to an isolated tribe of jungle folk who employed methods of psychology and inter-personal relations so astonishing that they might have come from another planet," wrote Kilton Stewart, introducing "Dream Theory in Malaya," surely one of the most remarkable documents in anthropological literature. According to Stewart (a trained psychoanalyst as well as an anthropologist), this tribe called the Senoi had created the kind of utopia that civilizations all over the world had tried and failed to build time and time again throughout history.

The Senoi claimed that their tribe, numbering approximately 12,000 when Stewart visited them, had not suffered a violent crime in several hundred years. Stewart observed for himself that "the absence of violent crime, armed conflict, and mental and physical diseases in their own society can only be explained on the basis of institutions which produce a high state of psychological integration and emotional maturity, along with social skills and attitudes which promote creative, rather than destructive, inter-personal relations. They are, perhaps, the most democratic group reported in anthropological literature."

What was their secret? Who were their leaders? According to Dr. Stewart, the key psychological and political practice that kept this remote Eden running smoothly was a community obsession with dreams, dream interpretation, and creative work or social relations based on messages from dreams. Each morning, the community would gather in a large hut and talk about their dreams of the previous night. The only leaders in the various communities that made up the larger tribe were the *dream psychologists* known as *halaks* (hah-LOCKS), who educated the children in the art and social system of Senoi dream work, who helped cement social relations by encouraging people to share the gifts and warnings they found in their dreams, and who led a kind of group consensus-gathering process based on dream work.

By drawing the whole community into a recognition of the intuitive, holistic, symbolic mode of consciousness exhibited in dreams, the *halaks* created what can be seen as a psychological and social counterbalance to the overly rational, analytic, instrumental thinking that dominates Western industrial civilization. Maybe we ought to meet in the morning at the local coffee shop, appoint a *halak*, and start dreaming up our own utopia! Sooner or later, every gathering of friends begins to talk about their dreams, and some pretty amazing things emerge. But people rarely know where to go with such a conversation. That's the time to say, "What we need is a good *halak*."

When we were children, our mothers were our *halaks*. Unfortunately, most of our mothers were trained to soothe our fears, not to encourage our explorations. Our society harbors a few false *halaks*—those who think that dream interpretations can be dispensed like astrological advice. Until our own society begins to adopt some of the features of the Senoi culture, those of us who cannot afford psychoanalysis must each be our own *halak*. This psychosocial role might become one of the growth industries of the 1990s and beyond, however, as the importance of inner guidance (and the need for psychological services for the broader population) becomes more evident.

altjiranga mitjina (**Aranda**)
The timeless dimension of dreams. [noun]

Now that psychophysiologists are beginning to study the uses of controlled dreaming as a probe of conscious states, and now that more has been learned about the role of dreams in creative inspiration and scientific problem-solving, neuroscientists have begun to look more seriously at the anthropological reports of cultures in which dreaming skill rather than the ability to invent material technologies is the primary source of the culture's power. The "primitives" of the Australian outback, for example, appear to have a relationship to their dream lives at least as intimate and intense as our relationship to our appliances and vehicles.

The Australian Aranda term *altjiranga mitjina* (allt-jeer-ON-gah mit-JEE-nah) was revealed to the West by Géza Róheim, a student of Sigmund Freud whose life's work was the application of dream theory to the anthropological inter-pretation of myth and folklore. In his work *The Gates of the Dream*, Róheim writes of "the eternal ones of the dream" who occupy a central position in Aranda mythology. The literal translation of *altjiranga mitjina*, "ancestor was," is a hybrid mental-temporal category that the Aranda contrast to the term for "now is"—what we would call "the waking present."

The *dreamtime* is the way some Western scholars translate the term, and it is understood to mean *a kind of eternal, pre-vious, mythical era—the time of the ancestors as well as the kind of time that accompanies the dreaming state of consciousness.* Those who understand a little about this concept insist that the

Aranda mean to say that there is *no* difference between the time of the ancestors and the time of the dream—in the other state of consciousness, time and eternity stand in a different relationship to one another than they do in waking life. The "old ones" are both the legendary figures who created the culture in ancient historical time and the kind of present-day personal symbol that a Jungian would call an archetype. And the life lessons that cannot be taught by any waking teacher, that can thus *only* be delivered in this eternity-within-dreamtime, are more than spiritual symbols, for they strongly influence the ethical and social behavior of those who haven't forgotten the meaning of the dreamtime.

Is the concept of *altjiranga mitjina* a vestige of preindustrial superstition? Or is it a fragment of a vast knowledge focused on the internal world of the mind rather than the external, material world? How primitive might our own civilization look to some powerful but spiritually unsophisticated invaders 40,000 years from now? Perhaps the destiny of our species is out in the physical world, in the countless stars beyond our mother-planet. Or perhaps it lies in the interior world, the one we carry around with us wherever we go and ignore most of the time—our own forgotten *altjiranga mitjina*. This kind of untranslatable word might be more appropriate to use in that other world: If and when you ever have a lucid dream in which you realize you are dreaming but don't know what to do with your knowledge, and if then some wise and powerful-looking figures begin to approach, they will probably appreciate your calling them by name.

The dreamtime isn't confined to our sleeping hours. If

you have ever been in an automobile accident, you are
familiar with the kind of time distortion in which you seem
to be moving in slow motion and your awareness expands to
take in many details in a short period of time. People who
have rushed into burning buildings or who have pulled
wounded comrades out of danger in combat also know
about the *altjiranga mitjina*. In sports, when an uncountable
number of physical and mental events combine in a short
period of time to create a perfect catch or dive, athletes
experience their own kind of *altjiranga mitjina*, a time in
which their own "old ones"—their coaches and teachers—
seem to be with them in a kind of time outside of time. The
more we are able to name and recognize these special states
of consciousness, awake or asleep, the more we empower
ourselves to call upon them when necessary. The next time
your car goes into a skid on an icy road, or you have an
opportunity to make a double play, or see a child darting
into traffic, the *altjiranga mitjina* might come in handy.

istiqâra (Arabic)
**A request for spiritual or practical assistance in the form
of a dream. [noun]**

English has words for "prayer" and "hope" and "concentration," but Arabic combines and transcends these three concepts with a word for *the psychospiritual art of solving problems
in your sleep: istiqâra* (is-ti-CAR-uh). The Moslem tradition
was built upon old foundations. For nearly a thousand years
(6th century B.C. to the 5th century A.D.), a large proportion

of the Greek population went to one of the 300 or more "dream temples," at which the god Asklepios was said to appear in special healing dreams to offer relief from illness. If that sounds esoteric and foreign, consider the curious fact that Asklepios is still honored by Western medical doctors, in that his *caduceus*, or serpent-twined staff, is the symbol of modern medicine! In ancient Greece, if a pilgrim seeking a healing dream arrived at the gate of the temple compound, he or she was required to sleep in the outer courtyard until Asklepios appeared in a dream. The god could be recognized by his snake-entwined pilgrim's staff. Pilgrims who received the dream invitation moved into the temple's inner compound—the *dormitory*. For the fortunate ones, another dream from the god would offer a diagnosis and prescribe a treatment.

The Islamic practice of *istiqâra* did not involve sleeping in a sacred place, but it did include the recitation of special prayers before sleep, coupled with a very strong expectation of an answer to a vexing spiritual problem, to be delivered in the form of a dream. Similarly, the stories of Jacob, Joseph, and Daniel in the Old Testament and the dream of Joseph in the New Testament, as well as the "night journey" of Mohammed, provide ample scriptural evidence of the use of dreams as vehicles for the transmission of divine knowledge.

In this pragmatic age, where practical assistance is usually more convincing than spiritual advancement, this word can easily be adapted to secular ends. Considering the fact that Niels Bohr's discovery of the atomic structure, Kekulé's discovery of the shape of the benzene molecule, and René

Descartes's discovery of the scientific method itself were all attributed by their discoverers to knowledge transmitted in dreams, there is ample reason to believe that systematic referral of aesthetic, scientific, interpersonal, and other secular problems to the unconscious sources of wisdom who speak through dreams might have very practical results.

The next time you are wrestling with your conscience, struggling with a design problem, musing over a creative project, trying to resolve something in one of your personal relationships, why not try *istiqâra?* Conversely: The next time someone asks you where in the world you ever came up with that bright idea, say you just used your *istiqâra.*

alam al-mithral (Arabic)
The world where images are real. [noun]

Two contemporary chroniclers of the dream realm, David Coxhead and Susan Hiller, in *Dreams: Visions of the Night,* had this to say of the world of images that can be approached through dreams, through visualization, and through that combination of focused intent and guided visualization known as "active imagination":

> In order to establish the reality of their spiritual experiences in dreams and visions, Muslim mystics were led to identify an exist-ent world of images, the *alam al-mithral,* halfway between the material world and the world of intellect. This world of images is not unreal. Henry Corbin, who has studied the *alam al-mithral* and written about it extensively, explains that affirming the exist-ence of the world of images should not be understood as a flight from what we have agreed to call reality but that, on the contrary, too facile a rejection of it may appear very much like a flight from

internal reality. The faculty of active imagination, or imaginative consciousness, by which one is able to enter this world should not be misinterpreted as fantasy. The world of images is not imaginary: one approaches it through a highly trained and specific "imagination," and the figures and images which inhabit it have an existence of their own....

The landscapes and figures of the world of images exist in a reality that has been visited by many, and for each it has had a "sameness." The visionary dreamer can, if pure enough in intent and provided he or she has reached a sufficient level of spiritual development, add to this world, or explore it further by means of heightened spiritual understanding. And because the faculty used is this "imagination," there can be no distinction between "creation" and "exploration," between "develop" and "identify." The world of images is a dream world which a number of dreamers may visit, and in which they are able to distinguish recognizable forms and images in the same act by which they create them.

What if this "world of imagination" is as real as we choose to make it, as mystics, artists, and inventors have proclaimed? Could it be that a scientific study of *the mental world that has not yet emerged into visible reality* but that has achieved a state of inner maturity might open and empower our culture the way knowledge of alphabetic writing transformed the world? Perhaps we need an alphabet of the *alam al-mithral* (ah-LAWM ahl meeth-RAWL). The way to change old beliefs is to honor new ones. If imagination is truly an undocumented human capability rather than a distraction of idle moments, then we should teach our children when we catch them daydreaming to honor the images and ideas, fantasies and scenarios that they conjure in the privacy of their *alam al-mithrals*, for these are safe internal rehearsal stages for actions that might be premature or dangerous to test in the external world.

Contemporary psychologists have begun to discover the power of visualization. Olympic athletes now do exercises in which they envision themselves in the act of performing the perfect high-jump or pole-vault. People with certain illnesses visualize their bodies fighting back their infections. Scientists and engineers try to see solutions in their mind's eye. The growing legitimation of visualization techniques in sports, medicine, and the arts is a sign that our culture is building a bridge between the world of the concrete and the world of imagination. The next time somebody asks you where you ever came up with that bright idea, tell them that you found it in the *alam al-mithral.* When you catch your child or student in the act of daydreaming, mention that the *alam al-mithral* can be useful, if he remembers to bring something back from it. And when somebody catches you in the act of daydreaming, you can say, "Don't bother me! I'm exploring the *alam al-mithral.*"

bilita mpatshi (Bantu)
Blissful dreams. [noun]

In English, we have a special word for terrible dreams—*nightmares*—but we don't have a word for *blissful dreams, high dreams, happy dreams, positive dreams.* The Bantu-speaking people of Africa call blissful dreams *bilita mpatshi* (bee-LEE-tah mm-POT-she), and in one segment of our society the word has passed into the argot of an American subculture. Winifred Kelergberger Vass, a scholar of Afro-American cultural linkages, traced the origins of many words to be found in Afro-American slang back to their Bantu roots. The word that Kelergberger Vass found in America is still used in some sections of America that were settled by the descendants of Bantu-speaking slaves. *Beluthahatchee* is defined as a "legendary, blissful state where all is forgiven and forgotten."

The first step toward empowering positive dreams is to acknowledge them when they appear. If you experience one of those *blissful dreams where you wake up feeling energized and refreshed*, tell your friends you had a *bilita mpatshi* (if you favor the original Bantu), or tell them you experienced a *beluthahatchee* last night (if you prefer to respond in the Afro-American equivalent).

kekau (Indonesian)
To awaken from a nightmare. [verb]

A dream of paradise is a pleasant experience, but a thousandfold more blessed is *the sensation of awakening from a hellish nightmare*. When you are chased or tormented by slobbering demons across an endless, boiling plain, you have *no* alternative to waking up.

The degree of reality attributed to dreams seems to vary widely from culture to culture, and thus the importance attributed to nightmares can vary widely as well. For one mysterious example, in the high country of Laos, folklore includes legends of nightmares that can actually kill their victims.

Indonesian nightmares might not have been as dangerous as the Laotian kind, but the relief of awakening is important enough to rate a word: *kekau* (keh-COW). You'll think of this word the next time you turn around and see the demons gaining on you, only to be rescued from that hellish place and transported back to your cozy bed at home. Now that you know the name for that "Thank God it was only a nightmare" feeling, you can murmur "*Kekau*" to yourself, in an appropriately thankful fashion, mindful of those poor Laotian victims, perhaps doomed to flee forever, one half-step ahead of the slobbering demons.

This word can be extended metaphorically to include waking experiences as well. We need a word to describe the moments when a "waking nightmare" or a string of bad luck takes a turn for the better. Every spell of bad feelings or misfortune reaches a turning point, after which the terrible experiences are remembered with the kind of hazy feeling of unreality we associate with nightmares. These moments also indicate a kind of *kekau*.

séntak bangun (Indonesian)
To wake up with a start. [verb]

The Indonesians must place a relatively high value on awakening, for they have at least two words for waking up from a state of sleep. *Kekau* is the word for the act of awakening from a nightmare, and *séntak bangun* (SEHN-tock BONG-uhn) is the word for *awakening with a start*. The experience of awakening suddenly, with a brief, intense, muscle spasm often accompanied by a startling dream of falling, is a worldwide phenomenon that occurs as the result of human physiology. Medical authorities attribute the mental sensations to an artifact of a kind of benign epilepsy-like seizure where a bunch of nerve cells that ought to be quiet suddenly fire spontaneously. Evolutionary biologists hypothesize that this reflex could be a holdover from our distant past, when our forebears slept in trees, and when a sudden awakening might be a very handy thing if you slipped out of your sleeping perch. Newborn babies, when startled, respond in a similar manner, called the Moro reflex. Who knows? *Séntak bangun* might be one of those words that comes down to us from earlier, prehuman languages.

rêve à deux (French)
A mutual dream or shared hallucination. [noun]

According to conventional wisdom, we can *describe* our dreams, but we cannot *share* them. Dreams, in this worldview, are unalterably private and individual events. But conventional wisdom isn't the only kind, especially when it comes to the world of dreams. The phenomenon of *the shared or mutual dream* has long been known and analyzed in Hindu, Buddhist, and Shamanistic traditions, and there is enough folk-understanding in the West for the French to have a word for a perception, dreaming or waking, of an "unreal" event that is shared by two or more people: the *rêve à deux* (REHV-ah-dueh). Of course, Western scientists still have a problem verifying the reality of these experiences, since it isn't possible (at least through Western methods) for a third party to enter the dreams of two other people to ensure that they are identical. However, the advent of the discipline of transpersonal psychology and the use of lucid dreaming as a scientific probe of dream space has begun to uncover ways to verify this phenomenon.

Verification, in the scientific sense, might not be the best tool for evaluating the phenomenon of *rêve à deux*, for many spiritual traditions regard this state of consciousness as one that points to a higher, ineffable reality, and as such is not subject to the kind of verification demanded by Western science. In a sense, the act of analyzing a *rêve à deux* might destroy its truest meaning. Reality is a fragile thing that can sometimes be destroyed, rather than strengthened, by gross attempts at verification. The playwright Tom Stoppard put it this way, in his play *Rosencrantz and Guildenstern Are Dead*:

> A man breaking his journey between one place and another at a third place of no name, character, population, or significance, sees a unicorn cross his path and disappear. That in itself is startling, but there are precedents for mystical encounters of various kinds, or to be less extreme, a choice of persuasions to put it down to fancy; until—"My God," cries a second man, "I must be dreaming, I thought I saw a unicorn." At which point, a dimension is added that makes the experience as alarming as it will ever be. A third witness, you understand, adds no further dimension but only spreads it thinner, and a fourth thinner still, and the more witnesses there are the thinner it gets and the more reasonable it becomes until it is as thin as reality: "Look, look," recites the crowd. "A horse with an arrow in its forehead! It must have been mistaken for a deer."

Is unrealistic love a *rêve à deux*? Were Romeo and Juliet the victims of this kind of mutual delusion? Consider the "dream" of two people who join together to start a business. If it grows into a successful enterprise, they are praised as visionaries. But if they file bankruptcy, it seems as if their dream was a *rêve à deux*.

ngarong (Dyak, Borneo)
A secret helper who appears in a dream. [noun]

Wouldn't it be wonderful if a marvelous helper could appear in your dreams and offer guidance, inspiration, even suggestions for creative works? Strangely enough, this idea seems to crop up in many cultures and eras. Scientists, artists, musicians, and diplomats have reported instances in which their greatest works were apparently given to them in dreams, sometimes by mysterious "helpers."

One of the most well-known instances of dream helpers was noted by Robert Louis Stevenson, who confessed that many of his works, including the celebrated *Case of Doctor Jekyll and Mister Hyde*, were created by a workshop of dream helpers he called Brownies. In a little-known essay entitled "A Chapter on Dreams," Stevenson explained a bit more about these Brownies, or "Little People":

> The more I think of it, the more I am moved to press upon the world my question: Who are the Little People? They are near connections of the dreamer's beyond doubt; they share in his financial worries and have an eye to the bankbook...they have plainly learned like him to build the scheme of a considerable story and to arrange emotion in progressive order; only I think they have more talent; and one thing is beyond doubt, they can tell him a story piece by piece, like a serial, and keep him all the while in ignorance of where they aim. Who are they then? And who is the dreamer?
>
> Well, as regards the dreamer, I can answer that, for he is no less a person than myself...and for the Little People, what shall I say they are but just my Brownies, God bless them! who do one-

half my work while I am fast asleep, and in all human likelihood, do the rest for me as well, when I am wide awake and fondly suppose I do it for myself. That part which is done while I am sleeping is the Brownies' part beyond contention; but that which is done when I am up and about is by no means necessarily mine, since all goes to show the Brownies have a hand in it even then.

Brownies is a word with too many other connotations. The Word *ngarong* (nn-GAH-rawng), used by the Sea Dyak tribe of Borneo, is perhaps more apt. Every member of the Dyak culture fervently wishes to have a *ngarong*, but only one out of several hundred is chosen. Like the helpers who appear to Iroquois and other Native American dream workers, the *ngarong* announces itself in a dream. It is up to the dreamer to search through the village and surrounding countryside on the next day and wait for an animal or plant or even a rock to announce itself by drawing the seeker's attention. If it is a python, for example, that person never hunts pythons again and sets up a secret shrine in the family compound, where offerings can be made. In return, the *ngarong* appears in dreams to help the dreamer out with problems in waking life.

This word will come in handy for creative people who never seem to know how to answer the perennial question "Where on earth did you get that idea?" Simply tell people that your *ngarong* gave it to you! Think of your *ngarong* as a dream mentor, an inner adviser who responds to your requests (as in the practice of *istiqâra*), a kind of interior equivalent of a *halak*.

CHAPTER EIGHT

Spiritual Pathwords

The Map, the Territory, and the Mystery

> The traveller who finds his road blocked by a river will use a raft to reach the opposite shore, but, this shore once reached, he will not carry the raft on his shoulders while continuing his journey. He will abandon it as something which has become useless.
>
> Alexandra David-Neel, *The Secret Oral Teachings in Tibetan Buddhist Sects*

> Fishing baskets are employed to catch fish; but when the fish are got, the men forget the baskets; snares are employed to catch hares; but when the hares are got, men forget the snares. Words are employed to convey ideas; but when the ideas are grasped, men forget the words.
>
> Chuang Tzu

*L*anguage is the road to God, but words are the tools of the Devil. The map is not the territory. Terms may be used, but none of them are absolute. Don't bite my finger, look at where I'm pointing! Language collides painfully with paradox when words are used to direct people to the realm of spiritual matters. Possibly more blood has been shed throughout the centuries over differing interpretations of holy scriptures than over all the mercantile or territorial disputes combined. The Tibetan epigram quoted above, if applied to language, has a two-fold implication: Language can be the raft people travel on to get to the other shore. If we are ever to transcend our animal origins and aspire to our angelic potential, it will be through the correct understanding of the words to be found in the world's great spiritual teachings. But if the Buddhists and others are correct, we must abandon the raft or we will truly never arrive. Ludwig Wittgenstein, the Western philosopher of language, likened words to a ladder that must be abandoned once the mind has used them to ascend to metaphysical heights.

Christians, Jews, Moslems, and Hindus use the words of their ancient scriptures to learn of their higher nature and find the right way to live. Buddhists use words to defeat language and trick the mind into letting go of its own illusions. Sufis and Cabalists use double meanings, metaphors, anagrams, and other word tricks to convey the esoteric teachings embedded in exoteric scriptures. Animists use words to name and honor the living spirits that dwell in the world. Shamans use words as magical power objects, to propel the mind and spirit into the underworlds and upperworlds. And Taoists just let words flow by, like everything else, remembering to lay down their nets when their fish are caught. If there is one thing that all the world's different spiritual traditions agree upon, it is the necessity of both using words and then abandoning them when they have served their purpose.

From the Old Icelandic language spoken by the Norsemen to the Bantu spoken by African tribes, every culture that has left its mark has contributed something unique to the treasure house of theological semantics: The Tibetans tell us of the *bardos* between the worlds; the Moslems use *waq'f* to clarify the legal relationship between God and mortal property-owners; Indonesians know a special kind of discourse that can be carried out only with a person who is dying (*alkin*); and Koreans recognize a certain stubborn human trait as the cause of suffering (*won*). These and other terms in Arabic, Bantu, German, Hindi, Icelandic, Indonesian, Lakota, Sanskrit, and Tibetan point to spiritual or metaphysical notions that are at the same time alien and familiar to Western minds: While the terms might be foreign, the experiences are as intimate and familiar as our very souls.

The words on the following pages can be pointers, rafts, ladders, keys to spiritual worlds you've never imagined. Don't forget to leave them behind when you reach the other shore.

waq'f (Arabic)
Property given to God. [noun]

In Moslem countries, the act of "making a *waq'f* " (rhymes with "dock," with an "f" at the end)—*the giving of property to God*—is considered to be legally legitimate as well as religiously meritorious. The *Sharia*, the legal commentary on the Koran, the Moslem scripture, legitimates the act of deeding property to the Divine. At one time, over 70 percent of the country of Turkey was *waq'f,* a word that is used to refer to the property itself as well as the act of deeding it.

When a religiously minded American attempted to make a *waq'f* of some land in Northern California, the superior court of the state found that such an act is not legally binding because, in the words of the presiding judge, "Whatever the nature of the Divine, God is neither a person, natural or artificial, in existence at time of conveyance and capable of taking title." Due to the sensational nature of the community that inhabited the property and the flamboyant, passionate unorthodoxy of the grantor, Lou Gottlieb, the case was widely publicized when it was adjudicated, in the 1960s.

Gottlieb, a founding member of the popular folk-music trio The Limelighters, bought 31.7 acres in the backcountry of Sonoma County and vowed to deny access to no one. The result was Morningstar Ranch, the pioneering, notorious rural community of the hippie era. When a politically powerful neighbor objected to the open nudity, sex, drug taking, and violations of health and building codes, Gottlieb was ordered by the county to evict his guests. He refused, and when the county attempted to evict them, Gottlieb deeded the land to God. After he lost his case and the commune was dispersed, Gottlieb hit the road. At one point he found himself in a small town in India. When he mentioned his story, one of the natives said, "Oh, you made a *waq'f*," which was the first time Gottlieb realized that in at least one culture the idea was so common that there was a word for it.

Fascinating and controversial as the social experiment of Morningstar Ranch might have been, the legal obstacles to successfully giving your property to the Supreme Being are formidable. But if you want some excitement in your life,

Lou Gottlieb says, "I urge anyone who owns land and wishes never again to experience one instant of boredom, who wishes to live in a continuing state of elation, to deny no one access to that land and watch what happens."

tao (Chinese)
The way it goes. [noun/verb]

Tao (DOW) is the quintessential untranslatable word. Indeed, the first verse of the *Tao te Ching*, the classic Chinese book on the subject, warns that "the *Tao* that can be translated is not the *Tao*." Because many of the Chinese ideograms that convey the text can be used as either nouns, adjectives, or verbs, and the sequence of words is far more ambiguous than in nonideographic languages, the entire book, as well as the ideas conveyed therein, is open to a wide range of slightly differing translations.

It could also be said that the well-known first line means that "the *Tao* that can be expressed is not the eternal *Tao*," or "The description of the *Tao* is not the *Tao*," or "Words can be used to describe reality, but they are not sufficient for a complete description." Another way of looking at the problem of translating this word is to look at the historical evidence regarding the effectiveness of words as a medium for conveying wisdom: Mankind has so much more *knowledge* now than ever before of the kind that can be put into books, but *wisdom* remains as rare as it ever was. The kind of knowing that can be transmitted by words does not seem to have an effect on more profound kinds of knowledge.

What is this thing that eludes verbal description? Taoist sages assure us that mystery is part of it, but the *Tao* is nothing mysterious. A sage doesn't worship the *Tao*, but tries to harmonize with it. The *Tao* is all-encompassing, but it is not God. Translations tend to agree on "the way" as an English description of *tao*, and "The Way of Life" as a translation of *Tao te Ching*. But the Chinese resonances and implications of this single syllable are different, and perhaps richer than the English associations with "way." *Tao* can be used to describe the grain of a wooden plank, the drift of the galaxies, the unfolding spiral of a fern leaf, the way water spills, the way time passes, the way breath moves in and out, *the way things naturally happen if you leave them alone.*

Although Taoism does have an external form that resembles other religious systems, the essential philosophy is not religious; rather, it is beyond religion. That God (or gods and goddesses, or myriad universes) should come into being is part of the *Tao*. Important figures in Taoist history are not avatars, prophets, or messiahs, but have often been depicted as eccentric old hermits, vagabonds, beggars—simple folk who led unorthodox but uncomplicated lives. Although modern civilization makes it harder to lead an uncomplicated life, the *Tao* has not ceased being the *Tao*, and it is still possible to harmonize with it through art, actions, or artful nonactions. The existence of a sprinkling of best-selling books like *The Tao of Physics* or *The Tao-Jones Averages* indicates that our national psyche may be ripe for homegrown Taoism. Next time you catch on to the *Tao* of something, do the Taoistic thing . . . *don't* talk about it.

bonga (Santali, India)
Spirit of place who must be dealt with. [noun]

When Europeans came to the North American continent, the tribal hunting-and-gathering civilizations found it astounding that these powerful new invaders didn't regard the earth as a living entity. These newcomers found their spiritual power in spired buildings instead of the land upon which they built their structures.

As the great machines and cities established dominion, the old spiritual connotations of specific places were forgotten and paved over. In those few pockets of old-style agricultural society that continued to exist into this century, the beliefs—and languages—of these stubborn survivors furnish a glimpse of how the world must have looked before people started seeing it as a machine. In certain villages north of Calcutta, along the edge of the Ganges, for example, the people known as Santals still remember the importance of paying attention to the *bongas* (BON-gahs)—the local spirits of the place.

A delightful book by W. G. Archer, *The Hill of Flutes: Love, Life, and Poetry in Tribal India,* has this to say of the Santals and their place spirits:

> [Underneath the sun, beneath the clouds] bongas or spirits roam, and only by coming to terms with them can Santals be happy.... The third and most significant bonga territory is the village itself, its fields, houses, trees, hills, rocks and air. Here reside the *Sima* or boundary bongas, the *Bir* or forest bongas, *Buru* or mountain bongas, *Dadi* or spring bongas and *Khuntut* or tree-stump bongas.... Each dwelling contains an *Orak* or house bonga. All these bongas are "spirits of particular places," which the spot itself has

> partially suggested. Other bongas... have a much wider role and
> special places provided for them. Inside each house, a tiny com-
> partment, known as the *bhitar*, contains the *Abge* bongas—the bon-
> gas of the sub-clan to which the particular householder belongs....
> All these bongas are, in a special sense, a Santal creation.... Their
> prime concern is with Santals only. Indeed, to the bongas, Hin-
> dus, Muslims, Christians or the British simply do not exist.

Do you always stub your toe on that exposed tree root
in your backyard? The local tree *bonga* might be telling you
in its own way that it requires propitiation for your continued habitation on its turf. Or is it a piece of mislaid sidewalk
that trips you up? Could it be a *bonga* trapped underneath,
yearning to breathe free? When you move into a new house,
take some time to get acquainted with the local Orak. See
the *land nám* entry, later in this chapter, for more information on sanctifying your neighborhood. And when you sleep
by a stream or spring, by all means honor the Dadi and ask
them for beneficial dreams. It's time to get beyond the simple recognition of "good vibes": Let's bring the *bongas* back
into our lives! Get the kids in your neighborhood some
peanuts and mineral water to feed the friendly local spirits,
and organize a *bonga* hunt today!

bardo (Tibetan)
The plane between death and birth. [noun]

"Merrily, merrily, merrily, merrily, life is but a dream," goes
the nursery-school mantra. Is it true? For Buddhists, the
whole point of life is the realization that those things to
which we cling most desperately—life, love, youth, beauty,

our physical bodies, our existence as separate conscious entities—are actually illusions. Buddhist doctrines proclaim that each individual is fated to undergo a cycle of births, lives, deaths, and rebirths, until he arrives at the moment of enlightenment when the illusions are seen for what they are and the shining void behind them becomes visible.

Psychoanalyst Carl Jung spent years in scholarly studies of Buddhist doctrine because he was blazing a Western path toward the liberation from self-delusion that is promised by Eastern scriptures. This quest brought Jung into contact with a Tibetan manuscript that was over a thousand years old, the *Bardo Thödol*, known to scholars in the West as *The Book of the Great Liberation*, or, more popularly, as *The Tibetan Book of the Dead*.

The *Bardo Thödol* is a guide through the trials and tribulations—and illusions—of the after-death plane; it is recited to the corpses of the newly dead, to help them see the "clear light of the void" and deal with the illusory demons and deities along the way—projections of their own mind that beckon the ego toward rebirth into the world of illusion. Jung and other depth psychologists saw profound psychological insights in the Tibetan doctrine of "samsaric projections," and in the way the *Bardo Thödol* counsels the departed soul to neither fear the wrathful illusions nor yearn for the sensual projections, because they are all delusional structures created by the disintegrating ego (itself a delusional structure).

The word *bardo* (BAR-doh) is a particularly apt candidate for adoption into the everyday lexicon, for its meaning is not restricted to the storm of illusions that occur on the several after-death planes, but can apply to *any situation of radical transformation in which the psyche is buffeted between fear and longing*. Indeed, half a century after Jung discovered W. Y. Evans-Wentz's translations, Timothy Leary and associates published an American update that was meant to be read not to corpses but to living people who were undergoing an LSD "rebirth" experience. Jung and Leary both saw the power of the metaphor beyond its original cultural and religious context. A contemporary Buddhist commentator, Chögyam Trungpa, puts it this way in *The Tibetan Book of the Dead*:

> "Bar" means in between, and "do" means island or mark; a sort of landmark which stands between two things. It is rather like an island in the midst of a lake. The concept of bardo is based on the period between sanity and insanity, or the period between confusion and the confusion just about to be transformed into wisdom; and of course it could be said of the experience which stands between death and birth.

Trungpa is saying that you don't have to suffer the "big death" to benefit from an understanding of the *bardo*—transitional—state of mind. What use could a contemporary Western urbanite find for a word like *bardo*? A brief inspection of all the turbulent transitional situations in everyday life yields a wealth of possibilities: How about the postdivorce *bardo*? The teenage identity-crisis *bardo*? The incredibly severe hangover *bardo*? If you can see the clear light of the void while you're jammed into a rush-hour subway car with an assortment of demons, tempters, wrathful deities, and blissed-out beings, perhaps you'll be able to emerge from tomorrow morning's commuter *bardo* with a whole new kind of insight.

Here's another way to look at unemployment: "I'm in the between-jobs *bardo*." Although you might think of this word as esoteric and metaphysical, it can actually be a very useful everyday tool. By naming the place of potential clarity amidst apparent confusion, one can safely traverse a territory that otherwise would be very frightening. It can help us deal with confusion, rather than flee from it, wherever we encounter it.

adjal (Indonesian)
Predestined hour of one's death. [noun]

In the biblically mandated lifetime of threescore and ten years, there are 365 times 70—25,550—days. Most people find that number slightly shocking: It just doesn't seem like enough sunrises to constitute a lifetime. Indeed, the only real certainty in life is that every living being has a date with the unknown, and only suicides, psychics, and the condemned are able to predict with any degree of precision what that date will be. The Indonesian language has a word for this very significant, very personal part of the mortal calendar, and perhaps it is the only appropriate term to use when someone has died too young, too tragically, too unexpectedly: "There's nothing you can do when your *adjal* arrives." We have a word for birthdays, but no word for life's other bookend. Doesn't *adjal* sound better than *death day*?

land nám (**Old Icelandic**)
The sanctification of new land by mythologizing it. [noun]

In the old days, before it was paved over, the surface of the Earth was alive with invisible sites of power. From the *bongas* of India to the nature spirits and sacred springs of North America, people developed relationships with a spiritual landscape that coexisted with the inert external geography of their environment. To the Norsemen of 9th-century Iceland or the Navajo of the North American Southwest, the very features of the land were invested with sacred energies. In Western religious tradition, the notion of "the Promised Land" has loomed large in spiritual and political history of the Middle East. Such spiritual powers most often did not derive directly from the geography but were a function of a cultural group mind, concentrating its spiritual force on that particular area long enough for the old myths and legends to emerge from the land in their latest adaptive form. For example, consider the large number of Catholic churches that were built on sites where ancient or even prehistoric stone monuments had stood—the Chapel of the Virgin of Guadalupe, for example, near Mexico City, visited by hundreds of thousands of pilgrims each year, was the site of pilgrimages to the corn goddess long before the Spanish arrived.

Some cultures felt that the process could be expedited. Why wait for the myths to emerge from the neighborhood when you can project them onto it? According to mythologist Joseph Campbell:

The Norse, who in the ninth century A.D. settled uninhabited Iceland, mythologized the raw landscape. *Land nám* ("land claiming or taking") was their technical term for this way of sanctifying a region, converting it thereby into an at once psychologically and metaphysically symbolic Holy Land. And the Vedic Aryans on entering India, thirteenth century or so B.C., performed the same work upon the landscapes of the Indus Valley and Gangetic Plain. "The Kingdom of the Father," we have just heard, "is spread upon the earth and men do not see it." *Land nám*, mythologization, has been the universally practiced method to bring this intelligible kingdom to view in the mind's eye. The Promised Land, therefore, is any landscape recognized as mythologically transparent, and the method of acquisition of such a territory is not by prosaic physical action, but poetically, by intelligence and the method of art.

One of the tasks facing men and women as individuals on the verge of the 21st century is the remythologization of their lives; as communities, we face the task of remythologizing the new landscape that the industrial and postindustrial revolutions created and that have shaped our lives. The world has changed too fast recently, and in unprecedented ways; new myths are needed to encompass new ways of experiencing the universe. But old models no longer seem to apply to the environment. The new landscapes of our lives are often interior landscapes of new ways of thinking and communicating, rather than exterior landscapes of mountains and rivers. Sanctification begins at home, and home for many isn't filled with magical springs and holy mountains, but is a more synthetic landscape of artifacts and technological processes. Who is to say that refrigerators and driveways don't have spirits, that skyscrapers don't have *bongas*? Urban legends and new kinds of rituals are part of the process of *land nám* (lawnd-NAHM), in which the new world of high rises and satellite dishes is being integrated with the older power stories.

It's a good word to use to redirect the conversation when it degenerates into long technical arguments about how the world is going to hell in a technological hurry. You can always stop the dialogue dead in its tracks by remarking: "Sometimes I think that nothing less than a global *land nám* might be the only effective prescription for our collective spiritual dilemma."

dharma (Sanskrit)
Each person's unique, ideal path in life, and knowledge of how to find it. [noun]

What is my place in the universe? What is the best way to live my life? And how do I find the true answers to the previous questions? The world's spiritual traditions have been built upon the human impulse to seek such answers. The Sanskrit word *dharma* (DAHR-muh) serves as an essential clue to these mysteries for billions of people who adhere to the Hindu or Buddhist traditions. It might have powerful resonance for many in the West as well, however, no matter what their religious preference might be. The standard dictionary definition of "the virtue of adhering to one's duty," or Nancy Wilson Ross's "the path which a man should follow in accordance with his nature and station in life," in *Buddhism: A Way of Life and Thought*, simply do not convey the direct message of *dharma*.

In the Hindu cosmology, the universe is a vertiginously

vast place, populated by uncounted trillions of sentient beings, demons, and gods who are continually being born and dying, on time scales stretching from threescore and ten for a mortal lifetime to 300,000 billion years for the whole shebang to recycle. When faced with the simple question of what it all means, a human can feel pretty puny in such a big scheme of things, and thus decisions about how to live might be made from the despair of ultimate powerlessness. *Dharma* is there to be discovered, however, and it is the answer for the individual up against something too gigantic to comprehend. *Dharma* means to be yourself as fully as you can be, acknowledging that each human consciousness is a unique, precious experiment in finding the way to the essential truth. It can also mean, as it does in the Buddhist tradition, the teachings and practices that can lead to self-realization.

Jack Kerouac, the writer whose best-seller *On the Road* brought the Beat Generation to the attention of the general population in the 1950s, used the word in one of the senses it might be applied in the West when he entitled a novel about restless, nonconformist truth-seekers *The Dharma Bums.* It is similar, in some senses, to the Christian term *gospel*, but it is inherently nonsectarian. To seek ways of learning and following the *dharma* does not mean blind acceptance of this god or that doctrine; it is, rather, an acknowledgment that the right way to live one's life will lead to the enlightenment of all sentient beings and a declaration that each human being has a unique opportunity to discover that essential truth.

talkin (**Indonesian**)
To whisper instructions to the dying. [verb]

In the West, spiritual concerns about death are centered
on the afterlife, and religious precepts concentrate on how
people ought to live in order to achieve the right kind of
afterlife. In the East, the Hindu and Buddhist traditions also
concentrate on the question of how to live in order to
achieve a propitious incarnation. But what of the state of
transition? What can be said to a dying person that can help
make the experience a positive one? In the Western tradition, last rites either are ceremonial or are vehicles for con-
fession and absolution. In recent years, however, with the
advent of the hospice movement, more and more people
are attempting to find answers to the question of how to
help people through the process of dying. Many instances
of carefully and sensitively prepared death instructions have
resulted in experiences in which the dying persons reported
feelings of great peace and a sense of meaning, right up to
the final moment.

Many in the hospice movement argue that our sanitized,
euphemized culture tries to ignore the most fundamental
fact of life, and that deliberate ignorance results in a great
loss of a prime spiritual opportunity. The very existence
these days of such a place as a hospice, where people can
go to die with dignity and meaning, is an important step in
the right direction. But we need a word for the kind of communion that living and dying people can share; the introduction of a word for the kind of special dialogue that can

help ease the anxieties of the dying might change our society in a positive way.

In Indonesia, a kind of religious and psychological speech known as *talkin* (TALL-keen) refers to the act of whispering instructions in the ear of the dying. In the Indonesian tradition, these instructions are also read at the end of the funeral service to remind the deceased about the proper answers to offer when questioned by the angels of death. No matter what religious tradition one adheres to, isn't it possible to prepare and perform a final act of kindness and spiritual assistance that would be consonant with sound psychology as well as sectarian beliefs? Perhaps we need to learn how to converse with the dying. Perhaps we need our own form of *talkin.*

won (Korean)
Unwillingness to let go of illusion. [noun]

In Eastern religions, the cause of suffering is seen to be "ignorance" of the evidence that desires and hungers and thirsts are part of an illusion. In Western religions, the cause of suffering is seen to be an inability or refusal to accept the reality of Jehovah or Jesus Christ or Allah. Even if people understand that there is a way out of their spiritual dilemmas, they often seem unable or unwilling to let go of the very illusions that keep them enthralled to suffering. The Koreans use the word *won* (WAHN) to refer to this perverse and paradoxical trait. Wendy Doniger O'Flaherty, a scholar of Eastern spiritual practices and an expert on the notion of illusion, puts it this way:

The cause of rebirth—excessive attachment to the ways of the world—is also the cause of the failure to see through the deception and illusion of the world. The qualities that make the soul cling to rebirth or to illusion are vividly encompassed by a Korean word, *won*, which has a cluster of meanings, including resentment, ingratitude, regret for lost opportunities, and a knot in the stomach; this state of the soul results from being poorly treated or unappreciated while living or from any of the many situations covered by the rubric "to die screaming." The unwillingness to let go, the inability to leave things unavenged and unfinished, is the drive to rebirth.

This word is another way of looking at what we in the West call "sin." But *won* is far too useful to restrict to a theological context. We all know people who suffer from *won*: those who are incapable of letting go of an old love affair, the days of past glory, memories of a happy or unhappy upbringing. By recognizing *won* in ourselves, by knowing that holding on to the illusions of the past is a natural human tendency, we make it easier for ourselves to let go of what we once cherished in order to grasp a new, perhaps less illusory, kind of reality.

Wundersucht (German)
Passion for miracles. [noun]

There are two strains of feeling within every religion. On the surface, as it is understood by the masses of believers, is the teaching of the spiritual leader or godhead that proffers an explanation of life on earth, of the origin of the universe, of the meaning of existence, of the proper morality and ethics needed to conduct one's life. At the core of every religion is another strain, often deeply submerged, of mysticism, of direct experience of godhead, which often includes secret techniques for altering consciousness in order to directly experience the source spoken of by scriptures. On many issues, these two planes do not intersect, but on one matter—the fascination with and passion for miracles— both the exoteric and esoteric forms seem to agree. Except for the highest adepts, to whom miracles are just another form of temporal illusion, the majority of people seem to exhibit a hunger for the miraculous, whether it is through mystic union or the sacraments of the church.

The passion for miracles, which the Germans call *Wundersucht* (VOON-dur-sucht), is understandable: What good is a religion if it doesn't offer a way out of the dilemma of existence? Morality in the face of temptation is hard to accept without some miraculous promise or threat. The paradox of existence seems to call out for the miraculous. In this sense, *Wundersucht* is not limited to the religious impulse. We live in a time of *Wundersucht*. Advertisers rely on it. Some movies now consist entirely of special effects. If you are ever asked why people flock to theaters, to amusement parks, to charismatic political leaders, chalk it up to *Wundersucht*.

baraka (Arabic)
A gift of spiritual energy that can be used for mundane purposes. [noun]

The Moslem Sufi mystics have been known to achieve states of higher consciousness and religious grace through rituals involving prayer and dancing (the so-called whirling dervishes are an example of this practice). Upon occasion, a cone of spiritual energy is raised above the circle of dancing celebrants. *Baraka* (bah-ROCK-uh), which is related to the Hebrew word *baruch,* is used to describe this energy, and more generally the atmosphere created by a person or group of people who touch upon Oneness. It has been described as a kind of charisma or spiritual electricity, because it is a kind of power that seems to energize those who receive it, even when they return to their secular lives and mundane tasks. It is present, at times, in Mecca. It was created, for a moment, at Woodstock. It can be found in great cathedrals, mosques, and synagogues, and it can be found in the right storefront churches, jam sessions, and classrooms.

Baraka has many other, closely related meanings that distinguish it from mere charisma or what Christians know as "grace": It is sometimes considered a property or characteristic of persons, the way courage or kindness or strength are properties that vary from individual to individual. A person who seems to prevail against overwhelming odds, who produces positive contributions under adverse conditions, who rises to a position of leadership, is considered to possess a quantity of *baraka.* This state can also attach itself to objects, as described by the poet-scholar Robert Graves:

> *Baraka* is the Moslem sense of blessedness that attaches itself to buildings or objects after years of loving use by noble-hearted people. *Baraka* may seem a foolishly sentimental subject, but few practical people will deny that to break in a new guitar, typewriter or car and as it were humanize it, so that it never lets one down, takes a long time, even if one has used a predecessor of the same make

> for years previously. And a ship's engineer, particularly if he is a
> Scot, often achieves so friendly a relationship with his engines that
> they somehow continue to work after apparently irremediable
> damage.

Baraka can be bestowed, which is one of the reasons that
some religious communities often founder or stray after the
death of a spiritual leader whose *baraka* permeated the community during his or her lifetime. Your teenage son, the hot-
rodder, might someday achieve *baraka* from a set of metric
wrenches. The teacher who smiles, ever so slightly, directly
into your eyes at the moment you grasp a new concept is
passing you some *baraka*. It's a good word to know about
and a good thing to create, receive, and transmit.

ondinnonk (Iroquoian)
The soul's innermost benevolent desires. [noun]

To the Conquistadores and the Pilgrims alike, the spiritual
practices of Native Americans were dismissed as little more
than superstition. But those white people who learned
something about these ancient cultures before they were
destroyed discovered that many of these "savages" were far
more sophisticated than their conquerors in certain social,
psychological, and metaphysical matters. The fragments of
knowledge we still possess about the great Iroquois federation paint a picture of a society in which individuals were
believed to be guided by a benevolent inner spirit. Marc
Barasch, writing in *New Age Journal*, had this to say of the
place of this inner force in Iroquois society:

Many cultures have in fact used dreams as a central rite of communion, a way of harmonizing the individual with society and the palpable, if invisible, higher forces. The six tribes of the Iroquois Federation, for example, all had formalized dream rituals. A Jesuit missionary named Rageuneau, writing in 1649, noted that they believed that "a soul makes known [its] natural desires by means of dreams, which are its language." In a striking parallel to modern psychological theory, the Iroquois also believed that if this desire, which they called "Ondinnonk," were completely thwarted, the soul would revolt against the body and make it sick.

Centuries later, in Vienna, Freud rediscovered what the Iroquois knew as *ondinnonk* (ON-din-onk) when he said that the repression of the desires of the id, through the intervention of the superego, leads to neurosis. And Freud also pointed out that the sometimes monstrous creations of dreams are indirect evidence of the id's activities. But Freudian theory viewed the id as a monstrous thing that gravitates toward all sorts of antisocial pleasures and must be kept in line in the interests of civilization. To the Iroquois, the source of the soul's deepest desires was not a dank den of animalistic impulses but the font of wisdom and source of guidance. Like the id, it grows out of our deepest human nature, but unlike the id, its impulses are not pure aggrandizement of desires, but are more benevolent, life-centered, health-giving.

Perhaps we ought to adopt a word for the good kind of id and start doing things because we let our *ondinnonks* be our guides. Our id existed before Freud named it, but the act of naming, of assigning a living word to a phenomenon, is an act of empowerment. Knowing about the id and the struggle between infantile and socialized forces within us has enabled people to deal with these forces, and it has also contributed to the id's power. The same can be true of *ondinnonk*: When we start using a word for *the angelic parts of human nature*, in addition to those words we habitually use to refer to (and thus pay a kind of homage to) our more demonic forces, we will begin to see more power flow into those parts of our nature. Dreams are good messages to heed, and so are some waking impulses.

When you get the urge to do something good for somebody, especially if there is no chance that the person will reciprocate, it might not be your more cynical "survival instinct" or your satisfaction-hungry id that is talking, but your *ondinnonk*. Those small, altruistic impulses to pick up the garbage littering a meadow, to intervene when you see injustice, to volunteer your time to a worthy cause are messages. There is no telling where you might end up if you start listening to them. Go find a friend who is under a lot of stress, insist that she take the rest of the day off, and treat her to a picnic. If she asks whatever came over you, confess that you were just following the dictates of your *ondinnonk*. Whenever you get the impulse to abandon your usual urban-survival rules and actually stop and give some money to one of those beggars, you might consider paying heed to this impulse from your *ondinnonk*, for when you listen to it, you find that it begins to listen to you.

CHAPTER NINE

The Body Politic

Words and Social Action

Political activity among the Managalase is focused on the exchanges between affines and between their communities. A young man's primary exchange partners are determined when he or his sisters marry. Either their marriages reinforce existing alliances, as part of a cycle of marriage exchange, or they force members of the two groups to redefine their political affiliations. Consequently, marriage negotiations are very sensitive activities.... If any of the parties is publicly embarrassed during the proceedings, disruptions of political relations by quarrels, sickness, or open conflict are likely to result. To reduce this possibility, the Managalase politicians use metaphorical rhetoric ... to avoid direct confrontations during negotiations. Indirect discourse such as allegory also enables them to hide the substance of their discussions from others who are not directly involved. Furthermore, metaphorical rhetoric is a means of testing the opinions of exchange associates and partners before taking a public position on an issue.

> William H. McKellin, *Putting Down Roots: Information in the Language of Mangalase Exchange*

*P*olitical science is the realm of the practical: How do groups of people actually get things done? In the case of the Managalase, a linguistic community of approximately 6000 people in the Highlands of New Guinea, political arrangements involve the number of pigs to be included in a dowry. In the case of American politics, pigs may also enter the negotiations when one legislator pledges a vote on another legislator's bill in exchange for a commitment of support for one of his own "pork barrel" issues. In the jungle huts of the Managalase or the Capitol Hill cloakrooms of the U.S. Senate, all the subtle variations on direct speech—allegory, metaphor, rhetoric—are used as abstract means of achieving concrete ends. But political discourse is not limited to legislators or tribal leaders. Whenever a twelve-year-old girl prefaces a request for a favor from her older brother with a reminder about the night he came in late and she neglected to tell their parents about it, she is using indirect speech to achieve a political end.

Francis Bacon originally stated that knowledge is power. If he had studied the many ways in which different cultures use language tools as political instruments, perhaps he would have added the corollary "Words are political tools." By the time you journey to the realms of Indonesian and Javanese political awareness (*masa bodoa*), sample some tart Yiddish opinions about justice and law (*Kulikov* decisions), understand the Japanese attitude regarding private dedication to a cause (*tashinamu*), read what Poles think of enforced collectivization (*uspolecnić*) and unofficial political arrangements (*zalatwić*), learn the French term for those who habitually challenge the established political order (*contestaire*) or those who have friends in high places (*piston*), meditate on the Sanskrit phrase for volunteer work (*dharma bakti*), and gain insight into the Chinese notion of acting without taking action (*wei-wu-wei*), you will probably know more about the realities of political thought than you would learn in a semester of an orthodox political-science course.

Political words can refer to the acts of individual citizens or the directives of the state. In France, *dirigiste* actions involve the state in the nation's cultural affairs; in Germany, a person who makes a certain kind of brave but necessary political speech is said to possess *Zivilcourage*. Italians reserve a special pejorative, *qualunquismo*, for people who take a certain attitude toward politics; Javanese speak admiringly of people who possess social and political *insaf*. Political words can encompass grand metaphysical notions or gritty bureaucratic realities: The Hebrew phrase *tikkun olam* refers to a literally religious commitment to a kind of social action; the German *Papierkrieg* refers to one of the petty bureaucrat's most vicious weapons.

The difference between conflict and harmony, enlightened political discourse and anarchic riots, the lofty and the lowdown motivations of politicians, the roles of victim or shaper of history all depends upon how people respond to words. In the realm of political semantics, a little ammunition for the ordinary citizen goes a long way. The politicians have hogged all the good words like *filibuster, gerrymander,* and *pork barrel,* but now the constituency can fight back verbally with *Zivilcourage, piston, insaf,* and the others. In that sense, consider the words on the following pages to be a kind of survival guide for the political arena, from the level of the neighborhood to that of the state.

dirigiste (French)
State-directed society. [noun]

The idea that the state should play a central role in guiding the cultural aspects of a society as well as providing political and economic functions has been anathema to the culturally anarchic society that has grown up in the United States. Many people confuse the idea of state influence over cultural affairs with fascist or Marxist state control of political or economic behavior. In France, where the French culture, particularly the French language, has always been considered to be a precious national resource, the idea of state direction of cultural evolution is widely accepted. France is an example of what the French themselves call a *dirigiste* society.

In the United States, a melting-pot society, *the idea of state control of cultural affairs* has long been impractical as well as repugnant to the majority of the population; cultural affairs just seemed to take care of themselves as foreign ideas and foreign immigrants became "Americanized." But *dirigiste* thinking is beginning to find a following among those who believe that English should be the "official" language of the United States. The recent and continuing growth of a Spanish-speaking population has prompted people in several states to debate and vote upon the idea of "English-only" ballots and other state-supported attempts to influence this cultural aspect. Whenever a person who espouses conservative views about the role of government in people's lives begins to espouse positions that imply state control over cultural matters, it is proper to refer to their thinking as *dirigiste.*

The National Endowment for the Arts is a *dirigiste* institution. The very idea of applying for a grant from the government to write a book or create a sculpture is the essence of *dirigisme*. But culture isn't limited to the arts. If you want to totally derail a conversation, you can use this word the next time people are talking about whether your city government ought to fund a new stadium for the local professional football or baseball team. While your cohorts are debating domed stadia and Astroturf fields, just let them know that "the whole idea is terribly *dirigiste*, don't you think?"

contestaire (French)
A person who challenges the established order. [noun]

In 1986, a group of computer enthusiasts—a notoriously skeptical group—were addressed by former psychedelic guru Timothy Leary, whose slogan "Turn on, tune in, drop out" was one of the hallmarks of the American youth revolution of the 1960s. "I have a new slogan," Leary told the assembly: "Think for yourself, question authority." He had barely finished his sentence when a voice rang out from the back of the room: "I question that!" shouted one of the programmers. Leary was up against precisely the kind of person he had always been—what the French call a *contestaire*. A *contestaire* is not the same as a rebel, for rebels often become the establishment when their revolutions succeed. A *contestaire* would continue to ask troublesome questions after the revolution.

Every business, every school, every institution in which

there is an established order sooner or later comes into confrontation with *the kind of person whose stubborn questioning of authority sometimes leads to large-scale social transformations.* In its highest form, an American *contestaire* like Rosa Parks, the black woman who refused to move to the back of a bus and thus set off the civil-rights movement of the 1960s, is the kind of person who has helped social organizations evolve ever since the age of potentates. On the more negative side, no society can exist in a state of perpetual revolution, or the social fabric begins to unravel. The French have another, more well known word for a kind of social troublemaker—*provocateur*—that describes a person whose purpose is to discredit the opposition to the established order by drawing them into violent acts.

In May 1968, a remarkable set of events transpired in Europe, in America, and in China. This word comes from the French version of that global youth revolution. During that fateful month, the French endured a series of upheavals in Paris that were more violent than the American student protests but less earth-shaking than the Chinese Cultural Revolution, both of which were occurring simultaneously. The French call it *les événements de mai '68 à Paris,* and that is where the word *contestaire* originated. The word can be used to make a fine but sometimes important distinction. The next time somebody talks about going on strike or engineering a takeover or provoking a test case, and somebody else suggests that the troublemaker is a *provocateur,* that is the time to speak up and say, "No, she isn't a *provocateur.* Au contraire. She is a *contestaire.*"

dharma bakti (Sanskrit/Indonesian)
Volunteer work for one's country. [noun]

In Indonesia, there is a special phrase, derived from two Sanskrit words, that describes the notion of volunteer work for
one's country, a notion with spiritual undertones: *Dharma* (see
chapter eight, "Spiritual Pathwords") can be loosely translated
as "the true spiritual path a man should follow in life, the true
knowledge of how to attain enlightenment," and *bakti* can be
loosely translated as "devotion"; *dharma bakti* (DAR-muh-
BAHK-tee) conveys the idea that *a period of volunteer work for the
good of one's community is not only a good thing for the community
but an essential element to the spiritual development of the volunteer.*
The Indonesians felt so strongly about this idea that they
adopted this phrase of Sanskrit origin; perhaps Americans
ought to follow the Indonesians in this practice.

The Peace Corps and Vista were started in the United
States in the 1960s in response to the need for a secular volunteer mechanism by which Americans could commit
themselves to a period of community service in this country and the rest of the world. The idealism of young college
graduates at that time, coupled with the real need around
the world for their skills in medicine, agriculture, and engineering, created a means by which the privileged could
repay the human community for their good fortune, gain a
kind of education in how things work in the real world, and
make friends for the U.S.

Political and cultural trends in America tend to run in
decades-long cycles: Youthful, nonsectarian, community-

minded, spiritually grounded volunteer zeal has been unfashionable for almost two decades, but it is entirely possible that the American generation of the 1990s will take up the word and the spirit of *dharma bakti* with renewed devotion. Let us hope that is the case, and when our own children ask us what we think they ought to do with their lives and we proceed to expound on success, happiness, and fringe-benefit packages, let's not forget to mention that *dharma bakti* isn't a bad idea when you are young and unencumbered and don't know yet what you want to do.

Zivilcourage (German)
Courage to express unpopular opinions. [noun]

The principle of democratic government is founded on a fundamental social contract between interests that might be opposed to one another in all other matters—the principle that people have the right to express unpopular or even repugnant views. The specific strictures on the power of the government to limit freedom of speech, press, or assembly were built into the U.S. Constitution in order to guarantee a forum for the expression of political views from every portion of the spectrum. In the ongoing judicial interpretation of constitutional guarantees, particular attention has been paid to protection of the most unpopular views precisely because these are always the first voices—never the last voices—to be silenced. This guaranteed forum is just a mechanism, however, that can be powered only by the motive force of individuals who have the courage to speak their mind. Without people with the *Zivilcourage* (tsee-VEAL-koo-RAH-zheh) to speak for views they believe to be important, despite the unpopularity of those views, the forum is meaningless. Although the word is German, the potential, one would hope, is universal.

The terse definition of this word in *Cassell's Colloquial German* conveys something of its transcultural flavor: "The courage to express one's opinion in spite of unpopularity; there is no English equivalent. Note that the pronunciation of courage is as in French." There are two ways we can put this word to work: When you hold an unpopular opinion and nobody seems to be speaking out for the right side of an important issue, just mutter *Zivilcourage* to yourself and speak right up; and when others take this unenviable role, applaud their *Zivilcourage*, even if you don't subscribe to their political or social views. Whistleblowers—those people who lay their careers, reputations, and even their lives on the line to expose corruption or dangerous conditions in nuclear plants, toxic-waste disposal procedures, or defense contracts—exhibit this trait. Those people who stood up to the House Un-American Activities Committee during the McCarthy era also exhibited *Zivilcourage*.

Papierkrieg (German)
Complicated paperwork connected with making a complaint. [noun]

Have you ever noticed that warranties, insurance policies, and merchandise return policies are orders of magnitude more difficult to understand than credit applications or sales slips? When your mail service or telephone service or other monopolistic service is inadequate, have you noticed how many papers you have to fill out, sign, and mail? It is in the nature of a bureaucracy to protect itself from outside meddling, and in many institutions, the person who tries to file a complaint is bombarded with time-consuming, confusing paperwork. The Germans, wise to the ways of bureaucracies, have a word for the paper war that seems to be declared upon those who try to complain: *Papierkrieg* (pah-PEER-kreeg). Knowing the name of this phenomenon, unfortunately, does nothing to eliminate it. The only recourse the plaintiff has is psychological: If you don't let it bother you, success is more likely.

Papierkrieg is more deliberate than red tape. Bureaucracies produce red tape the way sawmills produce sawdust or cattle produce manure, as a natural and unwitting byproduct that has to be disposed of or waded through. *Papierkrieg* is a consciously created obstacle. It can drive you over the edge into rage, thus accomplishing its purpose of derailing you from your original intention of returning a faulty toaster or protesting an inaccurate tax assessment or fighting an unfair parking ticket. Whenever you stand in line only to be told that you have to fill out another form and get in another line, that is the time to mutter: "This is nothing more than *Papierkrieg*, but it won't stop *me*!"

wei-wu-wei (**Chinese**)
Conscious nonaction; the act of not acting. [verb]

There are many who witness the behind-the-scenes machinations of political power who would agree that the single talent that distinguishes great leaders is an ability to know the right time to refrain from saying or doing anything. The quintessential story, probably not apocryphal, about the profession of dispensing political wisdom for a fee concerned the businessman whose business required him to deal with the federal government. He hired an influential Washington, D.C., attorney to advise him, and paid a $5000 retainer. For this fee, the attorney told him: "Say nothing and do nothing." A few days later, the client, steaming over the high-priced and simplistic consultation, called the attorney and demanded to know what he meant. The attorney said: "I meant that you should say nothing and do nothing." In the next day's mail, the client received a bill for an additional $5000.

Wei-wu-wei (WAY-woo-WAY) is a phrase that run-of-the mill politicians might not need but that all great leaders recognize, whether they know it or not. In this sense, the Taoist philosophers of ancient China speak directly to today's leaders of business and government around the world, for Lao Tze and his successors used the term *wei-wu-wei* to describe *a state of mind that accompanies the state of "acting by not acting."* It isn't enough to do nothing, you see: You must do nothing at the right time and for the right reason, which means you must have the proper frame of mind; and *wei-wu-*

wei is precisely the way you want to feel in crucial situations—alert but not tense, nonactive but not passive, relaxed but concentrated.

The next time you know it would be wise to stifle a comment in a meeting or resist the urge to issue a memo, take a deep breath, unfurrow your brow, take your hand off that keyboard or telephone, and let yourself *wei-wu-wei*. Procrastination is not necessarily a bad thing if it prevents you from doing something that would be harmful or counterproductive. When you have to tell somebody (or yourself) that doing nothing is the most significant option from a range of alternatives, don't forget to *wei-wu-wei*.

qualunquismo **(Italian)**
Attitude of indifference to political and social issues. [noun]

Many people are under the impression that the president of the United States is elected by a majority of qualified voters. In fact, only 29 percent of the eligible voters voted for Ronald Reagan in 1984. These figures mean that the "landslide victory" of 1984 was created by a small proportion of the population. There is no conspiracy, except a conspiracy of ignorance, that determines whether or not a few people determine how everybody is governed. This growing indifference to the political process might become the most deadly political threat of the 20th century. *Qualunquismo* (kwall-un-KEES-mo) is what Italians call this deadly anomie—an attitude of indifference, genuine or feigned, toward political issues.

The democratic revolutions of the 18th century were philosophically grounded in the radical new idea espoused by the English philosopher John Locke and others who held that there is a "social contract" between the government and the people. This was transformed into one of the pillars of the American Revolution: The government derives its power "from the consent of the governed." The perhaps fatal flaw in this brilliant new social and political philosophy has been the threat of apathy, where people give their proxy to whomever is in power by simply not caring. The word is derived from a satirical political journal called *L'uomo qualunque*, published after World War II, that espoused a position that led to the use of this term as a form of political epithet. Use it the next time somebody says, "Why should I vote? One vote doesn't matter," or, "I don't know about that political stuff—I leave it to the politicians." An appropriate reply in such instances would be, "That's nothing but *qualunquismo.*"

insaf (Indonesian)
Socially and politically conscious. [adjective]

While some people claim to be politically indifferent (see *qualunquismo*), others simply do not realize that their right to speak, worship, live, and assemble as they choose is something they must work to defend. Those who continue to participate in debates, campaigns, and elections, who contribute their time, money, and attention to the issues of the day, possess *a special and precious kind of social and political awareness* that the Indonesian-speaking inhabitants of Java call *insaf*

(EEN-sof). In their language, the word connotes enlightenment as well as awareness, for they understand that to be
aware of political events is also to be *enlightened* about the invisible roots of freedom and unseen pillars of daily life. This is
not a word to be bandied about, but one to be bestowed with
admiration. It is a word that ought to reflect everyday behavior, not just be trotted out for speeches and holidays.

When you are interrupted by a telephone or the doorbell
and somebody asks you to support a political candidate or a
cause you believe in, perhaps this word will come to mind.
It isn't easy to knock on strangers' doors because you believe
in an issue or a candidate. Invite one of those volunteers
inside, listen to what he or she has to say, make a contribution, and don't forget to say, "I really admire your *insaf.*"

masa bodoa (Javanese)
Sociopolitically passive and unaware. [adjective]

The Javanese use the Indonesian word *insaf* to honor those
who are socially and politically enlightened, and they use
the Javanese vernacular term *masa bodoa* (MAH-sah boh-
DOE-ah) to connote *those who are sociopolitically passive, whose
awareness does not extend past the mundane affairs of the household.* This is different from the feigned indifference of
qualunquismo, for the *masa bodoa* are people who truly don't
understand what is happening to them. In ordinary times,
the distinction between the politically aware and the politically passive is unimportant. In times of political turmoil,
however, the distinction becomes critically important. When

the time comes for a nation to decide whether it shall be governed by its citizens or by a small group of autocrats, the matter of individual awareness becomes a matter of national concern. Anthropologist Clifford Geertz, who observed Javanese villagers after a violent period of political turmoil, noted in *The Social History of an Indonesian Town*:

> The *masa bodoa* are sociopolitically passive, the flaccid, the unaware. The aware-unaware distinction was drawn therefore between those who were, relatively speaking, highly sensitive to the movements of national life (and particularly its political movements), who were, either as leaders or committed followers, caught up in them, and those who were, relatively speaking, more insensitive to them. These latter were not unaware of the drama of national politics in any simple cognitive sense...but in the sense that they were puzzled, unsure, and somewhat phlegmatic spectators of, rather than self-conscious participants in it. They might better therefore be called the (politically) unresponsive; their opposite numbers the politically responsive. The *insaf* had crossed an invisible psychological line between being subjects of an autocracy and being citizens, however abject, of a republic; the *masa bodoa* had not.

The future of the American republic might well depend on whether future generations lean toward the *qualunquismo*, the *masa bodoa*, or the *insaf*. The more these terms are used, the more likely that people will become aware of these crucial differences.

Kulikov (Yiddish)
Legal judgment made for pragmatic reasons. [adjective]

We have such phrases as "kangaroo courts," "common law," "lynch law," and other variants on the formal justice system.

But we don't yet have a phrase to characterize those *judgments that are made for pragmatic or political reasons rather than legal or judicial grounds.* We might adopt a phrase from the Yiddish and speak of *Kulikov* (COOL-ih-cough) law.

There's an ironic expression in Yiddish that translates: "That's a *Kulikov* trial." It comes from something that allegedly happened in a small town in Poland (or maybe Russia, or Lithuania, or Hotzenplotz) called, yes, Kulikov. This town was so small, it had only two tailors and one shoemaker. And the shoemaker went crazy (maybe because he was the only shoemaker) and killed someone. So they held a trial, and the shoemaker was found guilty and sentenced to hang. But we're talking about the town's only shoemaker here, so they hanged one of the tailors instead.

How often are productive secretaries and other competent support personnel laid off during cost-cutting sprees in corporations, while incompetent or unproductive executives remain, simply because they know where some bodies are buried, metaphorically speaking? *Kulikov* decisions might be the office-politics equivalent of *Kulikov* law. And in the area of family relations, don't parents sometimes resolve disputes in a manner that bears a closer relation to pragmatism than justice?

tikkun olam (Hebrew)
Spiritual and political reformation of the world. [verb]

In every religion, two opposing factions seem to emerge over the issue of the place of politics in the activities of the religious community—those who feel that politics are not the concern of a community whose focus is on a higher plane, and those who feel that nobody can serve God without attending to the needs of humans. The relationship between political and spiritual reformation of the world has always been a powerful source of dialogue and conflict within the religion of Judaism. The politically liberal strain of contemporary Judaism uses the phrase *tikkun olam* (TEE-coon OH-lahm) to refer to the obligation of Jews to work for peace and justice in the secular realm as part of their overall spiritual duty. In this sense, *tikkun olam* means "to repair or reform the world." The reasoning behind this is that spiritual goals can never truly be achieved as long as there is conflict and injustice in the world.

The phrase comes from a legend of the mystical Lubavitch Hassidic sect, which states that when the Creator first said, "Let there be light," the word was written with three characters—the *aleph*, the *vav*, and the *resh*—AOR. In subsequent days of the Genesis week, the scriptures leave out the middle letter, the *vav*. The interpretation of this is that in order to enable creation of an imperfect world, God had to shatter this immense original concept of light; therefore, we are settling for something that illuminates but is not the real thing. There are sparks of this original light in everything, however, and when all are united once more, the messiah will come.

Tikkun olam implies the joining together of all these sparks as part of each religious person's sacred duty, and thus directs the pious *to reform the political as well as the spiritual inequities of the world.* This is clearly more than just a political statement—it implies a systemic transformation in the way we live upon the earth and in the way we live with each other.

The concept sounds great. How could anybody disagree with the idea that helping reform earthly institutions is part of the duty of every religious person? The problems and disagreements begin when people attempt to define the nature of reformation. Fundamentalists like the Ayatollah Khomeini and Jerry Falwell, for example, both represent religious movements that very strongly believe in the reform of political institutions. Yet the kind of *tikkun olam* advocated by Islamic or Christian fundamentalists leads to very different visions of how societies ought to operate. And the "new age" transformationalists in our country have yet another vision of how the temporal world ought to be repaired. Yet this same term can be used to describe all three of these very different manifestations. Whenever somebody asks, "What do these people want?" in reference to one of the above-mentioned groups, you can reply, *"Tikkun olam!"*

tashinamu (Japanese)
To privately devote oneself to a cause or project. [verb]

Politics is perhaps the primary example of a human activity that has the highest goals and the basest methods of achieving them. While most people would agree that certain projects require a kind of cooperative institution in order to attain the highest good for the community—education, health and welfare, caring for widows and orphans, for example—most people would agree that the process of seeking, exercising, and holding the power to accomplish these altruistic ends has been known to engender some of the lowest, sneakiest, vilest behavior known to humankind. As the old saying goes, one should never watch legislation or sausage being made. In order to do good, it seems, one must often do some not-so-good things. Part of the problem is that politicians must spend more time publicizing their good works than they spend doing their community-minded good deeds. That's where the Japanese penchant for self-effacement and deference of individual achievement to group goals comes into play.

The Japanese word *tashinamu* (tah-she-NAH-mu) is especially favored in the Japanese culture. It means *to privately devote yourself to some project or goal, whether or not it will succeed, and whether or not you will be recognized for the effort.* In a spiritual sense, it is close to the Christian idea of a ministry. But the goals can be as simple as adopting a favorite park or trail and visiting it with a backpack once a week to clean up the trash that others leave. Or baking bread and giving it away. Or making telephone calls on behalf of a political candidate. This word can be used as an answer to several questions that were previously regarded as rhetorical. To the query "What can one person do?" you can reply, *"Tashinamu!"* To the query "Why should I bother if I won't be recognized or rewarded?" you can say, "Do it for the sake of *tashinamu.*"

uspolecnić (**Polish**)
Enforced collectivization; mandatory social work. [verb]

When this term is applied to objects and institutions, it is easily translatable as "to socialize or collectivize." When *uspolecnić* (oos-po-WECH-neech) is applied to people, its meaning is more difficult to pinpoint. The formal dictionary definition is "to induce to be active in social/welfare work." This is not social work as we generally define it in America, however. My informant remembers his high school years as being filled with *praca spoteczna* (prah-tah spo-WECH-na)—chores that every student in Poland was obliged to perform. One weekend, the students were instructed to meet at the site of an apartment complex that had been constructed not long before. The bulldozers had left quite a mess, and it was up to the students—under teacher supervision—to even out the mud piles and plant grass and trees. For each *praca spoteczna* fulfilled, the student would receive a signed card, which the teachers later collected. Failure to participate in these chores meant a stern conversation with the school director, and in some cases could lead to expulsion. Very often, these obligatory chores were planned for Sunday mornings—just about the time when families leave for Sunday mass. (This might not still be the case in Poland, since my informant finished high school before the events of 1980.)

In theory, of course, the purpose of such chores is to "societize" people, to integrate them into the socialist culture, to make them into active participants in a society where people take care of one another without regard to financial reward. My informant feels that this is a 20th-century version of the feudal system under which peasants, who lived on property owned by the local lord, were obligated to spend several days a week cultivating those lands.

Does this word have applications here? Although we are a capitalist society, many of our institutions—schools, churches, social organizations such as the Boy Scouts—tend to enforce "good citizenship," sometimes in a heavy-handed manner. Although it is a much more pervasive part of Polish life, our tots who are encouraged to sell cookies for the good of their organization or to spend their time performing charitable works for their church community are participating in a mild form of *uspolecnić*. Of course, since we aren't forced by the government, we tend to see it as "good citizenship." When athletes are required to participate in drug-abuse prevention programs and judges sentence offenders to a number of hours of community service, this is also *uspolecnić*.

piston (French)
A friend in a high place. [noun]

In English we have a phrase for it: "I have *friends in high places*" says that we are acquainted with prominent and influential people. In France they have a single word for this much-coveted and sometimes very handy kind of relationship: *piston* (piece-TAHN). To make a friend in a high place—*se faire pistonner*—is everyone's hope. In cases like this, where the English equivalent lacks the Gallic combination of cynical realism and elegance of expression, it might be better to adopt the word, as we have adopted so many others.

Whenever the son or grandson of the president of a company starts working "from the ground up," everybody knows that he is not just any copyboy or assistant buyer; he definitely has a *piston.* Ex-generals hired by the defense industry immediately after retiring from the Pentagon are not necessarily hired for their expertise; they simply have their *pistons.* And needless to say, most all celebrities automatically have *pistons.*

zalatwić (Polish)
Using acquaintances to accomplish things unofficially.
[verb]

The dictionary translation of *zalatwić* (zah-WHAT-veech) is accurate but terribly incomplete: "to settle, take care of, deal with something." A better translation would have to include some body language, specifically a sly wink, for this is the kind of "arrangement" that is best written with quotation marks. For the most part, it means *using one's acquaintances to accomplish something through unofficial channels, usually in exchange for a reciprocal favor.* Thus the idioms *zalatwić na lewo* (arrange something "on the left," or under the table) and *zalatwić po znajomo'sju* (arrange things through one's acquaintances). This can apply to something as significant as "arranging" an apartment to "arranging" a chunk of ham—both things not readily available through the Polish government-planned economy. The word is on the border-land between noun and verb. It can mean "to arrange" or it can refer to "an arrangement."

Perhaps a friend of yours works at a clothing store: She'll be glad to help you *zalatwić* a few pairs of pantyhose (by setting them under the counter when they come) and save you a potentially long wait in line, if you (who work at a travel agency) would be willing to help her arrange those two sleeping berths on the July 19th train from Kraków to Gdansk, a night train that is notoriously crowded. Shortages seem to be a fact of socialist life, and *zalatwićing* is in general a very practical response. Note the difference between this word and the French use of *piston*—a friend in high places. Your friend doesn't have to be in a high place to help you *zalatwić*; he or she simply has to be in a position to arrange a small favor. The Chinese, interestingly, seem to have a word that is a bit of each: *Guan xi* (gwan-SHEE) is a kind of clout and ability to accomplish things outside normal channels through a network of relatives and acquaintances (as in "My cousin's sister's boss can get that permit.").

In America, we use the word *juice* to approximate *piston* or *guan xi*, but we don't really have a word that approaches *zalatwić*, although who among us doesn't prevail upon his brother-in-law the car salesman for a special deal on a new convertible, perhaps in exchange for two Super Bowl tickets.

CHAPTER TEN

Toolwords

Technology and Worldviews

To a certain school of thought the dependence of thought on language appears a painful weakness. This school strives to overcome the weakness by means of a heroic effort whose great products are formal logic and the mathematical language of formulas as used in the exact sciences. This program is limited, however, by the fact that every formalized "language" must be interpreted in order to mean something—and the interpretation in turn requires us to use our ability to communicate; i. e., our "ordinary language." We therefore do not escape the problem of ordinary language; rather, we marvel that ordinary language can be made more precise through the use of that same ordinary language.

Carl Friedrich von Weizsäcker, *The Unity of Nature*

*L*anguage has always been the invisible partner of technology. Without linguistic instructions, all inventions would be one-of-a-kind items. The inventor of the wheel, for example, has been given too much credit. The one who truly deserves accolades for improving the lot of humanity is the first person who told somebody else how to build a wheel. Language, a tool for transmitting encoded information, was the abstract lever that allowed our antecedents to build upon the knowledge of others, to increase their store of knowledge with each generation, and, finally, to stop reinventing the wheel. In each case, symbols, communicated first by auditory and more recently by visual signals, were used to create the abstractions necessary for compressing ever-larger amounts of information into ever-more efficient codes.

Although every human culture has evolved a spoken language, not every culture has a true alphabetic system of writing. Alphabetic technologies were relatively recent inventions, and like other empowering technologies, they allowed those civilizations that adopted or developed them to dominate those that didn't. It was a bootstrapping process that spread throughout the world. Hieroglyphs and pictographs were refined and abstracted to alphabets, and in some parts of the world, alphabets were used to build more powerful thinking tools like logic, mathematics, and science. Eventually, the invention of printing presses made it possible for entire populations to participate in this empowering technology.

With each level of abstraction, language made increasingly more power available to individuals. The first level of empowerment came with the slow evolution of spoken language and the growth of an oral tradition that undoubtedly began with hundreds of thousands of years of prehistoric hunter-gatherer societies and ended up creating agricultural civilization about 9000 years ago. Then the higher-level abstraction of alphabetic writing was invented about 3000 years ago, radically increasing the level of knowledge available to individuals as well as to entire cultures.

But the kind of hyperaccelerated scientific-technological

progress that led to the 20th century as we know it didn't begin until humans created the third level of linguistic abstraction: tools for generating and determining the validity of knowledge. Science dominates so much of the modern environment that few people ever think of it as a kind of language or thought tool, or suspect that it was first and foremost a way of thinking about the world and is actually a relatively recent invention. Indeed, a kind of linguistic lag has developed, for science and technology have progressed at an increasingly accelerated pace, but language has not kept pace. The proliferation of specialized jargon for technologists has helped create the gulf between the "two cultures," the sciences and the humanities. In this sense, adaptation of new words and worldviews from other languages might help us cope with the profound cultural and psychological effects that have been wrought by technology. And we can have *fun* with technology, albeit abstractly, for once.

One of the social changes that science and technology have brought to human civilization has been a kind of unspoken social contract between technologists and the rest of the population. Plows and steam engines, alloys and antibiotics have made life easier, more interesting, more exciting, more safe and long, so ordinary citizens have given our modern Prometheans a blank ticket to make our lives whiter, brighter, and fresher through the miracles of modern science. But the awesome external powers harnessed by science and technology have not always been tempered by the controlling internal qualities of wisdom and ethics. The disasters at Three Mile Island, Chernobyl, and Bhopal revealed the dark side of technology. So did the space shuttle exploding before our very eyes. Medicines have side effects, and new biomedical technologies have brought us to the brink of frightening ethical crises. Suddenly, the unspoken social contract is undergoing renegotiation. And with new social arrangements comes the need for new words.

Our attitude toward tools in general is perhaps the most important aspect of our worldview that is undergoing renegotiation and revisioning. The Japanese concept of *hari kuyo* might come in handy here, if it can help make us more conscious of our personal relationships with our tools. The French revere their *animateurs,* and perhaps we ought to find out why. The German word *Fachidiot* can help us remember that technical expertise has its blind spots. The Navajo *Shimá* and the Latin *Gaia* remind us that Earth herself must be reckoned into our plans. These words, and others from languages as different as Hopi and Yiddish, can serve as tools to help us deal with the brave new world created by our other tools.

View this chapter as a toolkit for thinking about tools. And for laughing about our predicament when we have to. After all, when a *Fachidiot* thinks up a *Schlimmbesserung,* even *Shimá* can get *farpotshket*!

Fachidiot (German)
Excessively narrow-minded technical expert. [noun]

Some paleontologists assert that technical and occupational specialization is as old as the human species, but that it did not truly thrive until the birth of civilization: In order to irrigate the fields of the first agricultural communities in the Fertile Crescent, work crews (and overseers) were needed to dig ditches. Then, when the agricultural surplus allowed people to do something else besides scratching the ground and scouring the countryside for enough to eat, came the first building projects: ziggurats, pyramids, monoliths. That's where the stonemasons, architects, tax collectors, accountants, overseers, and laborers truly started specializing.

Now that we're beginning to notice how many of the miracles of modern science—from bug sprays to disposable diapers—are messing up the system we all live in (usually because of a ghastly side effect that wasn't foreseen by the technology's inventors, investers, consumers, and boosters), the German word *Fachidiot* (FAHCH-ee-dee-oat, where the "ch" is pronounced as in "loch") is ripe for pancultural adoption. The kind of person who can pack the transformers that hang on public power lines with a wonderful insulator like PCB, without realizing how toxic it will be to all the people who might step in it when it leaks, is only the most dangerous example of the many *narrow-minded technological specialists who cannot foresee the consequences of their work*, the kind Germans contemptuously call *Fachidiots*.

This word could be adopted globally to refer to the way technicians can mishandle affairs when they don't trust the concerns of nonspecialists. The way the nuclear accident at Chernobyl in the Soviet Union or the chemical disaster at Bhopal in India came about indicated that *fachidiotic* thinking was out of control. The designer of the disposable but nonbiodegradable device known as the Styrofoam cup was a

Fachidiot extraordinaire. But you don't have to be a technologist to be a *Fachidiot*: The word is appropriate in any instance when a person's degree of specialization causes a radical narrowing of focus and an inability to see the big picture. A *Fachidiot,* the exact opposite of a systems thinker, is a person who divorces the context and consequences from individual actions. Politically, the word refers not to those who believe the end justifies the means, but to those who are so concentrated on the means that they don't even think about the ends.

hari kuyo (Japanese)
Shrine for broken sewing needles. [noun]

Is the world a sacred vessel of wonder, in which even a stone or a pin is one of the visible faces of godhead for those who have eyes to see it? Or is the world a repository of inert resources to be used for the pleasure and aggrandizement of humans, a kind of cosmic supply depot? Is the purpose of a tool to extend human creative power or to dominate nature? In an important sense, our attitudes toward our tools reflect our spiritual attitudes. Some people value a tool as if it were inspirited, not for its monetary value but for its beauty and partnership in craft.

In the modern era, we as beneficiaries of the industrial and scientific revolutions have shared a largely unspoken agreement that "inanimate" nature, lacking flesh and spirit, can be regarded only instrumentally, as something to be used. In many nonindustrial cultures, however, a reverence for all existence, down to the humblest tool, is sometimes honored, an attitude that is often dismissed as a form of animism or pantheism. Is such a worldview "primitive"? Or is the merciless instrumentality of industrial civilization truly the more spiritually primitive belief? And does an undercurrent of native animism or pantheism run deep in our own society?

In Japan's Wakayama province, every village has *a special shrine where an interment service is performed for broken sewing needles.* The basis for this unique kind of temple is the belief that since the sewing needles died in the service of their owners and worked hard all their "lives," it is only fair that when they break they should be put to rest in a bed of soft tofu.

Such a ceremony could be dismissed as a silly superstition. But if you examine the beliefs of any master craftsman, you will discover a certain reverence for tools as worthy friends. The world-renowned Japanese temple carpenters, for example, spend much more time *sharpening* a tool than they spend making the cuts. The spirit of fine Japanese carpentry dictates that the planning and contemplation of a construction project should take much longer than the execution; in some cases, the carpenter lives on the site of a house or temple for at least a year, paying attention to the geography and the light, sharpening his tools, visualizing each cut, each piece of joinery, in his head, over and over again.

The concept of a *hari kuyo* indicates an attitude. At one point, when the mass-production era was in full swing, it seemed that such attitudes were obsolete. The renewed concern for "excellence" in the Western business community, however, signals an attempt to reawaken such an attitude on all levels of labor and management. With American and European corporate leaders falling all over themselves in a rush to emulate Japanese business management theories, perhaps someone will pay more attention to the less codifiable aspects of reverence for one's work. What else but a *hari kuyo* is the Baseball Hall of Fame or the Smithsonian Institution, where historical objects from Babe Ruth's bat to the Wright Brothers' plane are consigned to immortal storage?

How about that pair of beloved, well-worn slippers or that flannel shirt you can't bring yourself to throw away, even though it's falling apart? Certain objects of clothing, through faithful and memorable use, earn the right not to be thrown away. In this sense, many an attic is a kind of *hari kuyo*, filled with objects that are too meaning-laden for garage sales or garbage cans. The next time somebody catches you in the attic, wading through your memorabilia, and someone asks what you are doing, say, "I'm looking through the *hari kuyo*."

animateur (French)
A person who can communicate difficult concepts to general audiences. [noun]

Technology grows more complicated every day, but the general population is not becoming more literate. The result is that we are building more and more powerful machines, but fewer and fewer people can figure out how to operate them! That's where the new and growing role of *animateur* (on-eemaht-HER with "H" silent) comes in. The problem has been brewing for a long time, but the home computer revolution—or, rather, the failure of the home computer revolution—has brought it out into the general consciousness.

When the personal-computer boom started in the early 1980s, market forecasts were wildly optimistic. The professional prognosticators looked at the initial sales figures and predicted that every home in America would have a computer within a few years. But many of the machines that were taken out of their boxes during the boom years were put back in as soon as the new owners took a look at the instructions, which were often written in a technological dialect so specialized that they weren't even called "instructions." No, the stapled or spiral-bound book of technologese that accompanied the home computer had to be called "documentation," and it was often written by an engineer rather than a writer.

With the proliferation of underemployed writers, a successful new genre was born: books that explained the documentation that came with various computers. Of course, not all of these books were masterpieces of clear communication, but there were enough decent writers who had a grasp of this new technology to establish some standards. Now that the market has discovered the value of *a writer who can present complex scientific or technological information in an easily understandable form,* the *animateurs* (those who take dry material and "animate" it, or "bring it to life") will begin to make headway in the other areas where public understanding of important technologies is lacking.

The English word *popularizer* is too pejorative. *Animateur* should be applied with admiration to the kind of man or woman who can tell you in plain English how to operate your new fifty-button phone system. If more people used the word with enough pride, maybe we would all be able to figure out how to use the increasingly baffling new appliances that become available every day.

Shimá (Navajo)
Earth as mother. [noun]

Gaia [Greek]
Earth as an organism. [noun]

These closely related words from opposite ends of our planet might seem out of place in a chapter on technology, and that is precisely why they are here: It is time for technophiles to reevaluate the relationship between our tools and our environment. It is widely known that Native American spiritual beliefs regarded the planet as the literal mother of humankind. *Shimá* (SHEE-may) is the Navajo version of the *earth-as-mother concept*. And it is fitting that a Navajo word should be introduced into the English lexicon at a time when strip-mining and coal-burning power plants are despoiling the earth and air of the Navajo ancestral lands. The attitude that human technology is best suited for "the conquest of nature" dates back to the time of Sir Francis Bacon, who declared, in the early 17th century, that it was the mandate of human knowledge-seekers to "torture Nature on the rack" to induce Her to yield her secrets!

Certainly, technology has reaped many benefits for humankind. But many would say that the time has come to treat the source of those benefits, our planetary home, with more reverence. Wouldn't it be a refreshing change if, when a nuclear plant was being planned, a life-form was being created, or a chemical factory was constructed, the planners were to ask themselves what *Shimá* might think of it? They would prove themselves to be the very opposite of *Fachidiots*.

Resonating strongly with *Shimá* is the Greek *Gaia*, the name of the goddess of the living Earth. More than twenty years ago British biochemist James Lovelock proposed that the Earth's entire ecosystem was in fact a single living organism; for this hypothesis he chose the name *Gaia* (GUY-ah). The idea that our planet itself is alive was suggested as an explanation for the tendency of the Earth's lower atmosphere to maintain its temperature, oxygen concentration, and alkalinity within the narrow limits necessary for the sustenance of life. Lovelock presented compelling evidence that atmosphere and the terrestrial surface are part of an enormous self-regulating system that starts with cells, builds into organisms, collects into communities, and interconnects with others via ecosystems. If attention is energy, as certain sages have said, then perhaps we ought to put energy into the idea that we are part of one giant organism. Better to say *Gaia* than to say die.

koyaanisqatsi **(Hopi)**
Nature out of balance. [noun]

The Hopi, who live in the oldest continuously inhabited community in North America, have a word that is appropriate to the kind of situation that misapplied technology often creates. *Koyaanisqatsi* (coy-on-iss-COT-see) means "life out of balance." It also means "a way of life that is so crazy it calls for a new way of living." This word does not necessarily imply an indiscriminate condemnation of technology; if the Native American tribes had been vaccinated against smallpox, for instance, before the first Europeans showed up, the history of the New World might have been written in Algonquin instead of Spanish and English. But *koyaanisqatsi* is perfectly applicable to the kind of misuse of technology that creates ecological or human catastrophes. For example, whenever DDT or other insecticides are used indiscriminately, the very pests intended for elimination come back in force because the poison kills all but those who are immune (thus helping to breed an insecticide-resistant strain of insect) and also kills all the insect's natural predators. The hideous bustle of rush hour in megalopoli is *koyaanisqatsi.*

Antibiotics, which have saved millions of lives, have been misused to such an extent that there are now superbacteria that are virtually immune to all normal antibiotics. Hospitals have to be closed when they become overrun by these supergerms, and all the linen as well as the physical plant itself has to be steam cleaned. When artificial fertilizers render land infertile, when antibiotics breed killer germs, when unchecked growth of Sunbelt cities uses up underground aquifers that took millions of years to accumulate, the result is, unfortunately, *koyaanisqatsi.*

Schlimmbesserung (German)
A so-called improvement that makes things worse. [noun]

Consumers were mesmerized into decades of passivity by the magical words *new and improved,* but more and more people are beginning to question whether fast foods are any better than the slower kind, whether we want lemon-scented everything in our kitchens, whether we should consider ourselves social pariahs if the water in our toilet bowls isn't blue. We are entering an era in which people are beginning to question whether all problems can be solved by throwing technology at them. The time is ripe for that good old German word for *improvements that make things worse. Schlimmbesserung* (sh-lim-BESS-air-oong). While perfect for many egregiously inappropriate applications of technology, *Schlimmbesserung* is by no means limited to technological "improvements."

This word showed up a week before the manuscript was due in the form of an article by Jack Smith entitled "Is It Progress, or Just *Schlimmbesserung?*" in the *Los Angeles Times Magazine.* Another entry was bumped so this could be included, because we *need* this word, and we need it now.

Smith nominated the "diamond lanes" on Los Angeles freeways as a bureaucratic example of a *Schlimmbesserung.* The "diamond lanes," for those who haven't experienced Los Angeles freeways at rush hour, are reserved for buses.

All cars have to cram into the other lanes. Of this phenomenon Smith wrote: "I can't recall any public folly that has inspired more jokes, many of them very funny, than this wonderful notion that the way to ease traffic on the freeway during the rush hour is to close off one lane."

This word has a momentum all its own. Mention it in any group, and you will soon find that people can't resist offering their own suggestions. Some think that colorization of classic black-and-white films constitutes an open-and-shut case of *Schlimmbesserung*. People have mentioned heavily scented air fresheners, adjustable-rate mortgages, artificial lemon juice, and psychoanalysis as candidates for this label.

We can actually improve the quality of life for ourselves and future generations by introducing this word into common usage, especially among planners, designers, developers, engineers, bureaucrats, and policy makers. Our lives will be better when more people have the presence of mind to say, "Wait a minute! Let's reconsider this issue. It is clear that we are planning a *Schlimmbesserung*, not an improvement."

farpotshket (Yiddish)
Something that is all fouled up, especially as the result of an attempt to fix it. [adjective]

One of the most important linguistic categories of the technological age is the collection of terms that can be used to describe all the ways tools, machines, and systems can go *wrong*. Two terms from the military describe machinery or systems that have gone seriously awry: *fubar* and *snafu*. Apocryphal lexicography has it that *fubar* is an acronym for "fouled up beyond all recovery" and *snafu* is an acronym for "situation normal—all fouled up." (Of course, it is probable that military men used a word stronger than *fouled.*) But these are rather general terms. Technology requires precise terminology.

The Yiddish word *farpotshket* (far-POTCH-ket, rhymes with "tar NOTCH set") has the degree of specificity required by modern, complex technology, for it refers to *something that is all fouled up, especially through repeated failed efforts to fix it.* If Rube Goldberg was a repairman instead of an inventor, he would be a master of the art. When something minor goes wrong with your car, for example, and you attempt to repair it and turn the damage into something major, you can say that your car is *farpotshket.* In a political sense, the fall of Richard Nixon started out as a "third-rate burglary" that got all *farpotshket* when the White House attempted to cover it up. The word has a satisfying onomatopoeic ring to it, which adds emphasis: "That software was slightly buggy before your programmers tried to fix it, but now it is royally *farpotshket.*"

CHAPTER ELEVEN

Strange Memes

Language Viruses

Examples of memes are tunes, ideas, catch-phrases, clothes fashions, ways of making pots or of building arches. Just as genes propagate themselves in the gene pool by leaping from body to body via sperms or eggs, so memes propagate themselves in the meme pool by leaping from brain to brain via a process which, in the broad sense, can be called imitation. If a scientist hears or reads about a good idea, he passes it on to his colleagues and students. He mentions it in his articles and his lectures. If the idea catches on, it can be said to propagate itself, spreading from brain to brain. As my colleague N. K. Humphrey neatly summed up an earlier draft of this chapter: "Memes should be regarded as living structures, not just metaphorically but technically. When you plant a fertile meme in my mind, you literally parasitize my brain, turning it into a vehicle for the meme's propagation in just the way that a virus may parasitize the genetic mechanism of a host cell. And this isn't just a way of talking—the meme for, say, 'belief in life after death' is actually realized physically, millions of times over, as a structure in the nervous systems of individual men the world over."

Richard Dawkins, *The Selfish Gene*

*M*emes are what this book is all about: words that act like viruses, gestating in the primordial syntactic soup of one language before invading other linguistic communities, finding semantic niches, and propagating themselves from mind to mind until they have colonized an entire culture. The word was popularized by evolutionary biologist Richard Dawkins in the final chapter of his book *The Selfish Gene*. The premise of the book was startling enough—that humans and all other biological organisms are merely vehicles for transporting and propagating various genes, which compete with one another for representation in future populations by lending evolutionary advantages to the organisms that carry them. In his last chapter, Dawkins pointed out that certain *ideas* are propagated linguistically, and use minds and cultures the way genes use organisms and species; these ideas are the entities he calls memes, and words are the vectors that carry them.

Everyone has experienced a kind of mental invasion that is at once irritating and fascinating. This unwanted cognitive assault is closely coupled with a particular form of cultural communication, and the Germans call this obsessive thought-trap an *Ohrwurm*—a meme in the classical sense of Dawkins's definition. But there are other words in this chapter that are not such purely exemplary memes, but that might nevertheless have culturally infectious properties and that don't seem to fit into any of the other categories in this book. *Strange memes* are the words that fall into the cracks between the categories, the inhabitants of this book's *Zwischenraum*. As the entries in this book accumulated and fell into certain groups, I noticed how some of them stubbornly resisted categorization and was reminded of semanticist Korzybski's warning against mistaking the map for the territory. This chapter represents something more potent and elusive than "miscellaneous" words. Some of them have the potential to explode any categorization schemes we might try to impose on language and the world words describe.

People often mention the cliché about the seventeen words the Eskimos use for snow. Have you ever wondered about the truth behind the cliché? The answer, or at least part of it, can be found in the following pages. If your mind boggles at large numbers, you may never recover from your encounter with the Sanskrit word *kalpa*. Do you need a word for explaining inexplicable events? Look up *stam* and *davka*. When you see somebody hurt himself and don't know what to say, take a hint from the Swedes and exclaim *uffda*! These and other words from French, German, Hebrew, Navajo, and Scottish await you. Be careful. They might colonize your brain.

Gestalten (German)
Little wholes that make up larger wholes. [noun]

The methodology of every respectable science is to analyze the subject matter of chemistry, physics, or biology until the "fundamental particles" of that system are known. The payoff is very high for those who can see the world as a collection of different parts, so those of us who inhabit industrialized, science-based cultures tend to develop acute perceptions for parts, while neglecting the skill of seeing webs of interactions between the parts. However, a subtle shift has recently come to the world of scientific knowledge: The notion of *whole* systems has become fashionable.

Toward the beginning of the 20th century, the word

Gestalt (gehsh-TALLT) began to migrate from strictly German to limited English usage when a school of psychologists in Germany began to formulate concepts of perception and cognition based on pattern-seeking behavior; basic Gestalt psychology theory is based on the premise that all experience consist of *Gestalten* (gehsh-TALL-ten)—*integrated structures or patterns that must be apprehended as wholes rather than disconnected parts.* Gestalt perceptual psychology used optical illusions that depend on peculiarities of figure-ground relationships to demonstrate how visual *Gestalten* influence what we think we see. The famous silhouette that can look like either two faces looking at one another or an empty vase, depending on which element is seen as the figure and which is seen as the ground, is a visual demonstration of how the perception of *Gestalten* can affect one's interpretation of the perceived object.

In music, the pattern of notes that make up the melody is a *Gestalt* that is greater than the sum of its parts. In graphic design, the arrangement of visual elements in terms of figure-ground relationships that form *Gestalten* can increase the effectiveness of visual communication. In the life sciences, the dynamic interrelationships of all the different living participants in an ecosystem have become matters of paramount importance to biologists, ecologists, agronomists, and others who study the terrestrial ecosystem. Indeed, if the 20th century is the era of analysis carried to its extreme, the 21st century will undoubtedly become the era in which individuals and institutions will develop a heightened awareness of *Gestalten.*

Although this word is used in a rarified sense by social scientists and literary critics, it would serve us well as a general word: "Do you get the *Gestalten* of my intentions?" "She has a great sense of *Gestalt*." It's a word you would use when talking with your interior decorator or trying on a new outfit. It's a short and more specific way to designate any pattern that is more than the sum of its parts.

Zwischenraum (German)
The space between things. [noun]

The world was astonished when physicists revealed that matter consists almost entirely of empty space. Our eyes simply don't detect the lonely electrons, spinning in their distant orbits around tiny nuclei, separated by immense subatomic voids. Our perceptual system isn't the only factor that prevents us from paying more attention to the interstices, intervals, silences that Germans call *Zwischenraum* (ZVISH-ehn-rowm, rhymes with "dish in town"). There are plenty of spaces within our normal visual range, but we don't notice them most of the time, and for good reason: Survival on planet Earth requires constant concentration on the here and now, and thereby insures that our attention remains locked upon the doughnut, rather than the hole.

Whenever someone notices the space between things, important ideas can spring out of that fecund void. Western mathematics was transformed by the introduction of the concept of zero, imported by Moslem mathematicians from Hindu thinkers who originated the strange, indispensable idea of a number that is no number. The discovery of perspective—the portrayal of spaces between objects—by Renaissance painters heralded a new era in Western art; the importance of "negative space"—the eloquence of that which is *not* painted—is a hallmark of Zen brush-painting (and modern mass-media advertising).

Another way to see spaces between things is to adopt an auditory rather than a visual metaphor and pay attention to *silent* regions. What is music without silences? Anyone who has compared a live conversation to a transcript knows the value of the pauses, often barely perceptible, that punctuate the meanings hidden within verbal discourse. When Freud and Jung investigated the silent areas of consciousness, references to the "unconscious" became part of the popular vocabulary.

If you seek to probe the secrets of the human heart, decipher the mysteries of the cosmos, or just want to find out how much of what is happening in front of you is hidden from your awareness, look again at the spaces between the letters on this page, the intervals between the pickets in the fence outside your door, the sudden silences in crowded rooms, the myriad gaps and interruptions that keep everything from happening all at once in the same place: *Zwischenraum*. And when you are trying to tell people to "read between the lines" of the situation, tell them to direct their attention to the *Zwischenraum*.

Zwischenraum exists in every human relationship, in the form of what is not said when two people look at each other. In basketball, the part of the game where the action shifts from one team to another is known as the "transition game," and it is an example of *Zwischenraum* in sports. As individuals and as a culture, there is ample evidence for the hypothesis that we begin to know what is truly happening around us only when we develop a sensitivity to the emptiness between distinct events and episodes. Meditation is nothing other than an attempt to look objectively at the *Zwischenraum* between thoughts.

Elementargedanken (German)
Elementary thoughts of humankind. [noun]

To most people, fairy tales connote the very opposite of what an adult ought to spend time thinking about, and the term *fairy tale* is often applied colloquially to deride a statement that is clearly untrue. But the scholars of the 19th century who turned out to be the predecessors of the anthropologists and psychologists of the 20th century took their fairy tales quite seriously. It all started when Jakob and Wilhelm Grimm collected the tales that country people in Germany told their children, published them, and found themselves with a 19th-century best-seller on their hands. The rediscovery and publication of fairy tales turned into an international phenomenon. All over Europe and America, in the cities as well as the villages, people told and retold their children the stories of the Frog King, Rapunzel, Sleeping Beauty, and hundreds of others.

As the success of the German publication led to imitators in different countries, scholar after scholar in different nations reported that the same themes recorded by the Grimms existed in cultures as disparate as the Finnish and the Polynesian! Virtually identical themes popped up in literature and folklore in ancient Babylonia and modern Germany. Where did these stories come from?

One of the more intriguing hypotheses was that set forth by Adolf Bastian in 1868 with the publication of *Beiträge zur vergleichenden Psychologie,* cited by Marie-Louise von Franz in *Interpretation of Fairy Tales,* in which he proposed evidence that fairy tales did not originate in any single country, or even in several countries, but came from the human mind and are manifestations of a store of *basic motifs that are the built-in "elementary thoughts" of the human race: Elementargedanken.* In this sense he was following intriguing hints left by the Grimms, who wrote of the fairy tales as the remaining pieces of an "old wisdom"—a kind of knowledge that is no longer known—like "a broken crystal whose fragments you still find scattered in the grass." Bastian was also prefiguring the work of Jung, half a century later, that led to the concepts of the archetypes and the collective unconscious.

Is there an old wisdom that lives on at a subconscious level of our culture, a psychic transformation bomb buried deeply in the very tales we tell our children? Mythologist Joseph Campbell and poet Robert Bly have pointed out that the most consistent theme of these "fairy stories" is that of *initiation*—into a way of thinking that we abandoned, after half a million years, relatively recently in our cultural evolution. When we invoke the words that signal the introduction of numinous material—"Once upon a time"—do we open the channel for a transmission of knowledge that we know little about on the conscious level, yet perpetuate unconsciously? When we close our eyes in sleep, do we return to the *Elementargedanken* (elemen-TAR-gay-dawn-ken) mode—a way of thinking that isn't bounded by the same rules and restraints as those that govern waking rational thought?

You might not encounter them every day, but whenever you do encounter one of the great primordial themes of initiation, spiritual voyage, transformation, and integration, pay particular attention to the form of the *Elementargedanken* as they manifest in your dreams and thoughts, for these elementary ideas convey something personal about your present situation in life. C. G. Jung developed his theory of archetypes as a specific subset of personal *Elementargedanken.* They can be clues to your most important mystery, the quest to discover what your life means. And when a friend tells you that she dreamed of a caterpillar becoming a butterfly, you'll have the proper word to apply for these clues that float up from the deepest parts of our psyches: "Ahh, my dear Watson, an *Elementargedanken,*" you can reply.

Ohrwurm (German)
A tune or melody that infects a population rapidly. [noun]

If a meme is a cluster of semantic symbols that propagates through a human population in a social manner, similar to the way a gene is a combination of biochemical symbols that propagates through a human population in a genetic manner, a sudden, wildly popular new addition to "the top 40" can be seen as a kind of meme. When the medium of radio and the recording industry that grew up alongside it created a system for propagating musical themes through a population, a new phenomenon became possible—the "overnight hit." The idea of a hit isn't untranslatable, since most cultures have a word for the winner of a competition. But the idea of a tune, a melody, a combination of musical sounds that seems to be on everybody's lips at the same time, that spreads through a society as rapidly as a respiratory infection and that seems to invasively seize and occupy space in people's minds until they finally succeed in forgetting it merits a word of its own.

The Germans use the word *Ohrwurm* (rhymes with "door worm," where the "w" is pronounced like a "v") to denote these cognitively infectious musical agents. Whenever somebody complains to you that she just can't keep the latest pop tune from running through her head, tell her she can dispel it by calling it by name and by thinking about the original German meaning, which captures some of the mnemonically parasitical connotations of the word, for *Ohrwurm* literally means "ear worm" and is also used to refer to a kind of worm that can crawl into the ear.

kalpa (Sanskrit)
A cosmic measure of time. [noun]

Backed by all the technological armamentation of modern science and the efforts of the best scientific minds in history, Western cosmologists now estimate the universe to be approximately 18 billion years old. The latest theories about the decay of the proton—the last thing in the universe to give up the cosmological ghost—estimate another 100 billion years will pass until the universe runs out of all available energy and all matter is disintegrated or sucked into black holes. A hundred billion years sounds like a comfortable figure, measured against the human life span, but the Vedic cosmologists who invented the Sanskrit word *kalpa* (CALL-puh, rhymes with "tall, huh"), would laugh and chide today's astrophysicists for failing to think big enough.

According to the ancient Sanskrit traditions, human history is divided into four periods, or *yugas*. The first *yuga* is a golden age, but the second and third *yugas* become progressively less virtuous, more violent, and short-lived. The present *yuga*, the fourth by this reckoning, is the *Kali yuga*, a dark age of suffering, strife, war, and social disintegration. The present *Kali yuga*—there are many of them in the great cycle—began Friday, February 18, 3102 B.C., and will last 432,000 years. Together with the three previous, longer-lasting *yugas*, the great cycle, called the *Maha yuga* ("great *yuga*"), lasts for 4,320,000,000 years. One thousand *Maha yugas* constitute a single *kalpa*, which is a day in the life of the Demiurge god Brahma. At the end of the day, the god Shiva dances the universe into destruction until the next morning, when Brahma is born again.

If you are ever at a loss for words when you are trying to indicate a long period of time, when *eon* or *millennium* are inadequate, try *kalpa*. And if that isn't big enough, don't forget that only the earth and heaven are destroyed every *kalpa*, but when all the days of Brahma add up to a Brahma century, the earth, heaven, and all spheres of being whatsoever are totally reabsorbed into the ultimate void. Then another Brahma century of 311,040,000,000,000 human years begins again. So when the super particle-accelerator or ultratelescope of the 1990s yields new knowledge that pushes the estimate of the date of demise of the universe out to 300,000 billion years or so, don't forget to count your *kalpas*.

This word can come in handy for social situations, as well as for inducing cosmic vertigo. The next time your spouse asks when you want to go to your less-than-favorite relative's house for dinner, you can smile and say, "How about the *kalpa* after next?"

uovo di Colombo (Italian)
A simple, obvious idea that doesn't occur to the person who could use it the most. [noun]

A man once had a flat tire and got out of his car to change it. He carefully removed the lug nuts and put them down inside the hubcap of the flat tire. But the hubcap tipped over and dumped the lug nuts into the storm drain. As it happened, the car was parked in front of a lunatic asylum, and one of the inmates, who had been watching through the fence, suggested to the hapless driver that he remove one lug nut from each of the other wheels, put the spare tire on, and drive to a service station. Admiringly, the driver said, "I never would have thought of that! How clever!" To which the asylum inmate replied, "Well, I may be crazy, but I'm not stupid."

The point of this old joke is that sometimes the simple, obvious solution to a person's problem doesn't occur to him until it is pointed out. In the sense of the story told above, it is the intellectual equivalent of *esprit de l'escalier* (chapter two). The Italians call this kind of idea an *uovo di Colombo* (oo-OH-voh dee koh-LOM-boh), which is a literal translation of the phrase "Columbus's egg." The next time you rack your brains for *a solution that is right in front of you*, instead of excoriating yourself or looking sheepish when you are caught at it, simply exclaim, "What an *uovo di Colombo!*"

ocurrencia (Spanish)
Sudden, bright idea or witty remark. [noun]

In the universal language of cartoons, the event described by the word *ocurrencia* (oh-koo-REHN-see-ya) is depicted by a lightbulb over the protagonist's head, signifying the occurrence of a sudden bright idea. Like the Italian phrase *uovo di Colombo*, it refers to a sudden, perhaps important realization, but unlike the Italian version, *ocurrencia* doesn't necessarily refer to a solution that was obvious before it occurred to someone. If you are participating in a brainstorming session and the solution to the matter at hand occurs to you in a flash, you can say: "Wait a minute. I just had an *ocurrencia* that will solve all our problems." The word can be used as an intellectual equivalent of a bon mot, a "well-chosen thought," if you will. Although it is usually a positive exclamation, it can be turned on someone in a sarcastic manner by the proper use of a disparaging tone of voice. "What an *ocurrencia,*" intoned with proper sarcasm, can imply that the suggestion just voiced is not exactly the bright idea the originator obviously thought it was.

idée-force (French)
An idea that has an active, substantive power. [noun]

Ideas are at once the most worthless and the most powerful memes ever invented. The idea that the moon is made of green cheese, for instance, is considered by many people to have no use other than as an exemplification of human folly. On the other hand, the idea that people ought to love one another, as presented by Jesus Christ, or the idea that governments derive their power from the consent of the governed, as presented by John Locke and those of his admirers who framed the U.S. Constitution, seem to have a force of their own. The fact that certain powerful ideas can influence the course of history, or even amplify the power of the entire human species, is embodied in the French phrase *idée-force* (ee-DAY FORSE), which literally means "powerful idea."

Other examples of *idées-force* include the notion of literacy and education, the idea that people can pool their resources and develop a collective strength far greater than the strength of an individual, and the idea that the way one conducts one's life can affect the quality of one's afterlife. If an idea has power, it seems to sweep through a population like an infection, and if it is an idea whose "time has come," nobody and nothing can stop it from spreading and transforming civilization. Perhaps the most powerful *idée-force* is the idea that ideas have any power at all. Seymour Papert, a psychologist and computer scientist, put it this way in his book *Mindstorms*:

> What matters most is that by growing up with a few very power-ful theorems one comes to appreciate how certain ideas can be used as tools to think with over a lifetime. One learns to enjoy and to respect the power of powerful ideas. One learns that the most powerful idea of all is the idea of powerful ideas.

Certainly, the *idée-force* of the French and American rev-olutions of the 18th century was that all men are created equal. Communism was the great failed *idée-force* of the 20th century. The most powerful ideas, in terms of history, appear to be those that appeal to the heart as well as the head. It is not a term to be bandied about lightly. But you can lend power to one of these ideas when it comes along by identifying it with those other ideas that have shaped the course of events: "I think that candidate has come up with something far more important than a campaign slogan. It looks to me as if she has voiced an *idée-force*."

stam and *davka* (Hebrew)
Words for explaining inexplicable events. [verbs]

I asked Ari Davidow, formerly of Jerusalem, to contribute a few examples of Hebrew words for this book. Here is his first reply, verbatim:

"My two favorite Hebrew words are almost but not quite translatable. *Stam*, (shtahm) for instance, roughly means 'for no reason,' or 'because it's there,' or 'I'm doing it [it's being done to me] because that's the way the cosmos works.' An example (to note a common Jerusalem street scene): 'Yossi, why are you peeing on the sidewalk?' '*Stam*, Mother.'"

Then there is the redoubtable *davka*, which is philosophically similar to *stam*; but where *stam* implies some straightforward action, *davka* refers to the universal "everything is conspiring against me" theory. Why does it rain right after you wash your car? *Davka* (DOVE-kuh).

What both words have in common is a refusal to explain. Things just happen. It's a big, hostile universe out there, and being Israeli means not having to explain yourself (*stam*), and expecting the worst (*davka*).

Stam has an additional meaning, connoting surprise. For instance, there I was driving along the highway, when, just like that, *stam*, this bozo cuts in front of me. The tie-in, of course, is that there is no more explanation for some bozo cutting in front of my car than Yossi peeing all over the sidewalk. That's just the way things are, and don't bother me with silly questions."

uffda (Swedish)
A word of sympathy, used when someone else is in pain.
    [exclamation]

Every language has a word that is used when one is suddenly attacked by pain. *Ouch* is the most polite English word, and a variety of less polite words are used when people strike thumbs with hammers, hit their funny bones against furniture, or feel a sudden twinge of arthritis. But Swedish slang contains an onomatopoeic word that can be used as *a sympathetic exclamation when somebody else is in pain: Uffda* (OOF-dah) combines "Ouch for you" and "Oh, I'm sorry you hurt yourself." This is the kind of meme, like *Gesundheit*, that could catch on very quickly. The next time you have an opportunity, say it and see what happens. At the worst, you'll get a puzzled look. At best, you'll raise the compassion level in the world.

salogok (Eskimo)
Young black ice—one of many Eskimo ice-words. [noun]

When you mention that you are reading this book to somebody, you can be certain someone will say something about the existence of the famous seventeen words Eskimos have for snow. This was certainly the case during the research phase of this book, when so many of my friends and acquaintances independently mentioned the apocryphal seventeen words. It makes sense that inhabitants of Arctic regions would have a lot to say about snow. Although we aren't likely to find much use for them, wouldn't it be nice to actually know what those seventeen words are? The answer isn't hard to find, once you take a look at the ethnographic literature. But, like many cross-cultural legends and stereotypes, the truth turns out to be somewhat different from the common wisdom. The first surprise is that while there are plenty of words for snow, the real action in the Eskimo language is in the category of "ice." The second surprise is that the number of words for ice is much closer to 170 than seventeen.

Naturally, you can expect many of the Eskimo ice-words to refer to exotic conditions related to the extreme weather of Alaska and northern Canada, as well as fine distinctions that are important to Eskimos but which dwellers in more temperate climates don't seem to pay much attention to in everyday life. *Salogok* (SAH-low-gock) is one of the few that most people in the United States can experience on an early winter morning, for it refers to *a thin, nonreflective ("black") membrane of young ice.*

Following is a short sampler of Eskimo ice-words, quoted from "Eskimo Sea-Ice Terminology," an appendix to *Hunters of the Northern Ice*, a book on Eskimo ethnography by Richard K. Nelson:

> *Ugurugüzak*: grease ice; the earliest stage of freezing, causes wind ripples to disappear from patches of the water surface.
>
> *Maullik*: slush ice or ice rind; heavy development of grease ice, almost to the point of being nilas.
>
> *Pogazak*: slush or mush ice formed by grinding along the edges of ice pans, floes, or cracks.
>
> *Mogozak*: similar in meaning to the preceding terms, except ice may be solidly frozen. Eskimos sometimes refer to this as "file ice," because it is formed by the ice "filing" itself.
>
> *Migalik*: pancake ice; circular pieces of young ice, 1 to 6 feet in diameter, with raised rims; the shape and appearance result from rotation and collision with other cakes.
>
> *Salogok*: nilas, or black young ice; a thin, flexible sheet of newly formed ice which will not support a man, is weak enough to enable seals to break through it with their heads to breathe, and breaks through with one firm thrust of the *unaak*.

The same appendix lists 10 more words for ice age or thickness, 16 words for various conditions and states of ice movement (including the onomatopoeic *eyechektakok*: a crack that is pulsating or opening and closing), 50 words for sea-ice topography, and 7 words for phenomena related to sea ice and its movement. Following the reasoning that extreme and specific environments can generate large numbers of environmental nouns, is it possible that Angelenos someday will have the need for nearly as many words to describe freeway traffic conditions? Will subway commuters in Tokyo and New York develop a shared vocabulary to describe various states of discomfort in people-packed cars? Will San Francisco begin to add new words to the vocabulary in order to describe new American subcultures?

Do You Know an Untranslatable Word?

*T*his is the end of the book, but it doesn't have to be the end of our attempt to expand our language and worldview. You, the readers, can help with the next phase of the project. When I was performing the research for this book, I discovered that many people happen to have a strange meme or two stuck away in some cranny of memory. Do you know an untranslatable word that the rest of us ought to hear about? I can't pay you, but I will acknowledge the name of every person whose suggested word ends up in the next book on untranslatable words. (And don't forget that I may have found out about "your" word through other sources before I see your suggestion.) Tell me what is "untranslatable" about this word, in a paragraph or two. Try to include as much information as possible about references, whether it is a scholarly work or your great-grandmother, and some kind of guide to pronunciation.

Send your suggestions to:

Untranslatable Words
Jeremy P. Tarcher, Inc.
9110 Sunset Blvd.
Los Angeles, CA 90069

BIBLIOGRAPHY

Akimoto, Shunkichi. *The Lure of Japan.* Tokyo: Board of
    Tourist Industry, Japanese Government Railways, 1934.

Anderson, Beatrix. *Cassell's Colloquial German.* New York:
    Macmillan, 1980.

Archer, W. G. *The Hill of Flutes: Love, Life, and Poetry in Tribal
    India.* Pittsburgh: University of Pittsburgh Press, 1974.

Atkinson, Jane Monnig. "Wrapped Words: Poetry and
    Politics among the Wana of Central Sulawesi,
    Indonesia." In *Dangerous Words: Language and Politics
    in the Pacific,* edited by Donald Lawrence Brenneis
    and Fred R. Myers. New York: New York University
    Press, 1984.

Barasch, Marc. "A Hitchiker's Guide to Dreamland." *New
    Age Journal,* October 1983.

Basso, Keith H. *The Cibecue Apache.* New York: Holt,
    Rinehart and Winston, 1970.

Benet, Sula. *Song, Dance, and Customs of Peasant Poland.*
    New York: Roy Publishers, 1966.

Bishop, Morris. "Good Usage, Bad Usage, and Usage." In
    The American Heritage Dictionary of the English Language.
    New York: American Heritage Publishing, 1969.

Bohannan, Paul. "The Eloquence of Silence." *Science 80* (January-February 1980).

Brenneis, Donald Lawrence. "Straight Talk and Sweet Talk: Political Discourse in an Occasionally Egalitarian Community." In *Dangerous Words: Language and Politics in the Pacific,* edited by Donald Lawrence Brenneis and Fred R. Myers. New York: New York University Press, 1984.

Brown, R. and E. H. Lenneberg. "A Study of Language and Cognition." *Journal of Abnormal and Social Psychology* (1954):49.

Bryan, J., III. *Hodgepodge.* New York: Atheneum, 1986.

Buchanan-Brown, John, Jennifer Cang, John Crawley, Barbara Galushka, Gilman Parsons, Kate Williams, editorial panel. *Le Mot Juste—A Dictionary of Classical & Foreign Words & Phrases.* New York: Vintage/ Random House, 1981.

Buruma, Ian. *Behind the Mask.* New York: New American Library, 1984.

Campbell, Joseph. *The Hero with a Thousand Faces.* Princeton, NJ: Princeton University Press, 1949.

_____ . *The Inner Reaches of Outer Space: Metaphor as Myth and Religion.* Toronto: St. James Press, Ltd., 1986.

Capra, Fritjof. *The Tao of Physics.* Berkeley: Shambala, 1975.

Christopher, Robert C. *The Japanese Mind: The Goliath Explained*. New York: Simon & Schuster, 1983.

Codrington, Robert Henry. "Mana." In *Primitive Heritage: An Anthropological Anthology*, edited by Margaret Mead and Nicolas Calas. New York: Random House, 1953.

Coxhead, David, and Susan Hiller. *Dreams, Visions of the Night*. New York: Crossroad, 1976.

Daniélou, Alain. *Shiva and Dionysus: The Religion of Nature and Eros*, translated by K. F. Hurry. New York: Inner Traditions International, Ltd., 1982.

David-Neel, Alexandra, and Lama Yongden. *The Secret Oral Teachings in Tibetan Buddhist Sects*. San Francisco: City Lights Books, 1967.

Dawkins, Richard. *The Selfish Gene*. London: Oxford University Press, 1975.

Draeger, Donn F. *The Martial Arts and Ways of Japan, Vol. 1, Classical Bujutsu*. New York and Tokyo: Weatherhill, 1973.

Echols, John M., and Hassan Shadily. *An Indonesian-English Dictionary*. Ithaca, NY: Cornell University Press, 1961.

Eco, Umberto. *Travels in Hyperreality*. New York: Harcourt Brace Jovanovich, 1986.

Farkas, Emil, and John Corcoran. *The Overlook Martial Arts Dictionary*. Woodstock, NY: The Overlook Press, 1983.

Fire, John, Lame Deer, and Richard Erdoes. *Lame Deer— Seeker of Visions*. New York: Simon & Schuster, 1972.

Franz, Marie-Louise von. *An Introduction to The Interpretation of Fairy Tales*. Zurich: Spring, 1970.

Geertz, Clifford. *Peddlers & Princes*. Chicago: University of Chicago Press, 1963.

———. *The Social History of an Indonesian Town*. Cambridge, MA: M.I.T. Press, 1965.

———. *Person, Time and Conduct in Bali: An Essay in Cultural Analysis*. New Haven: Yale University Southeast Asia Studies, 1966.

———. *The Interpretation of Cultures*. New York: Basic Books, 1973.

———. *Local Knowledge*. New York: Basic Books, 1983.

Gerrard, A. Bryson. *Cassell's Colloquial Spanish Completely Revised*. New York: Macmillan, 1972.

Glendening, P.J.T. *Cassell's Colloquial Italian: A Handbook of Idiomatic Usage*. New York: Macmillan, 1980.

Grahn, Judy. *Another Mother Tongue: Gay Words, Gay Worlds*. Boston: Beacon Press, 1984.

Grambs, David. *Dimboxes, Epopts, and Other Quidams*. New York: Workman, 1986.

Grant, William, and David D. Murison, eds. *The Scottish National Dictionary*. Edinburgh: The Scottish National Dictionary Association Limited, 1974.

Graves, Robert. *Difficult Questions, Easy Answers*. New York: Doubleday, 1964.

Hall, Edward T. *Beyond Culture*. Garden City, NY: Doubleday, 1976.

Harrison, E. J. *The Fighting Spirit of Japan*. London and New York: W. Foulsham & Co., Ltd.

Hawken, Paul. *The Next Economy*. New York: Holt, Rinehart and Winston, 1983.

Heisenberg, Werner. *Physics and Philosophy*. New York: Harper & Row, 1958.

Hoover, Thomas. *Zen Culture*. New York: Random House, 1977.

Jameson, Fredric. *The Prison-House of Language: A Critical Account of Structuralism and Russian Formalism*. Princeton, NJ: Princeton University Press, 1972.

Japanese National Commission for UNESCO. *Japan—Its Land, People, and Culture*. Tokyo: Printing Bureau, Ministry of Finance, 1964.

Jung, C. G. "The Meaning of Psychology for Modern Man." In *The Collected Works of C. G. Jung.* New York: Pantheon, 1958.

Kauz, Herman. *The Martial Spirit: An Introduction to the Origin, Philosophy, and Psychology of the Martial Arts.* Woodstock, NY: The Overlook Press, 1977.

Kindaichi, Haruhiko. *The Japanese Language*, translated by Umeyo Hirano. Rutland, VT: Charles E. Tuttle Company, 1978.

Kundera, Milan. *The Book of Laughter and Forgetting.* New York: Knopf, 1980.

Laughlin, Robert M. "The Great Tzotzil Dictionary of San Lorenzo Zinacantán." In *Smithsonian Contributions to Anthropology.* Washington, D.C.: Smithsonian Institution, 1975.

Lee, Dorothy. "Being and Value." In *Primitive Heritage, An Anthropological Anthology*, edited by Margaret Mead and Nicolas Calas. New York: Random House, 1953.

Legge, James, trans. *Chuang-Tzu*, arranged by Clae Waltham. New York: Ace, 1971.

Levieux, Michel, and Eleanor Levieux. *Cassell's Colloquial French.* London: Cassell Ltd., 1980.

Lévi-Strauss, Claude. *Structural Anthropology.* New York: Basic Books, 1963–76.

Lewis, C. S. "At the Fringe of Language." In *Studies in Words*. Cambridge, England: Cambridge University Press, 1960.

Lincoln, Jackson Steward. *The Dream in Primitive Cultures*. Baltimore: Williams & Wilkins Company, 1936.

Lovelock, James. *Gaia: A New Look at Life on Earth*. London: Oxford University Press, 1979.

MacDonnell, Arthur Anthony. *A Practical Sanskrit Dictionary*. London: Oxford University Press, 1929.

Malinowski, Bronislaw. "Crime and Custom in Savage Society." In *The International Library of Psychology, Philosophy, and Scientific Method*, edited by C. K. Oeu. Totowa, NJ: Littlefield, Adams, & Co., 1926, 1967.

A Mandarin-Romanized Dictionary of Chinese with Supplement of New Terms and Phrases. 3rd ed. Shanghai: Presbyterian Mission Press, 1911.

Marett, R. R. *Head, Heart and Hands in Human Evolution*. London: Hutchinson's Scientific Books, Paternoster House, 1935.

Matsuwaga, Daigan, and Alicia Matsuwaga. *Foundation of Japanese Buddhism*, Vol. 2. Los Angeles and Tokyo: Buddhist Books, International, 1976.

McKellin, William. "Putting Down Roots: Information in the Language of Managalase Exchange." In *Dangerous*

Words: Language and Politics in the Pacific, edited by Donald Lawrence Brenneis and Fred R. Myers. New York: New York University Press, 1984.

Mitchell, Edgar D. *Psychic Exploration*. New York: Putnam's, 1976.

Nelson, Richard K. *Hunters of the Northern Ice*. Chicago: University of Chicago Press, 1969.

New Revised Velazquez Spanish and English Dictionary. Chicago: Follet Publishing Company, 1974.

O'Flaherty, Wendy Doniger. *Dreams, Illusion and Other Realities*. Chicago: University of Chicago Press, 1984.

Pacificon Productions, under contract to the California Department of Mental Health. *Friends Can Be Good Medicine*. Sacramento: State of California, 1981.

Papert, Seymour. *Mindstorms*. New York: Basic Books, 1980.

Pekelis, Carla. *A Dictionary of Colorful Italian Idioms*. New York: George Braziller, 1965.

Polak, Fred. *The Image of the Future*, translated and abridged by E. Boulding. San Francisco: Jossey-Bass, 1973.

Prabhavananda, Swami, and Christopher Isherwood, trans. *How to Know God: The Yoga Aphorisms of Patanjali*. New York: New American Library, 1953.

Róheim, Géza. *The Gates of the Dream*. New York: International Universities Press, 1952.

Rosaldo, Michelle Z. "Words That Are Moving: The Social Meanings of Ilongot Verbal Art." In *Dangerous Words: Language and Politics in the Pacific,* edited by Donald Lawrence Brenneis and Fred R. Myers. New York: New York University Press, 1984.

Ross, Nancy Wilson. *Buddhism: A Way of Life and Thought.* New York: Knopf, 1980.

Rosten, Leo. *The Joys of Yiddish.* New York: Pocket Books, 1970.

Sakai, Atsuharu. *We Japanese, Book III.* Yokohama: Yamagata Press, 1950.

Schlerath, Bernfried. *Sanskrit Vocabulary.* Leiden, The Netherlands: E. J. Brill, 1980.

Schwarz, Edward A. *Everyday Japanese.* Chicago: Passport Books, 1986.

Smith, Huston. *The Religions of Man.* New York: New American Library, 1958.

Smith, Jack. "Is It Progress, or Just Schlimmbesserung?" *Los Angeles Times Magazine,* 26 April 1987.

Steltzer, Ulli. *A Haida Potlatch.* Foreword by Marjorie Halpin. Seattle: University of Washington Press, 1984.

Stevenson, Robert L. "A Chapter on Dreams." In *The Works of Robert Louis Stevenson,* Vol. 16. London: Chatto and Windus, 1912.

Stewart, Kilton. "Dream Theory in Malaya." In *Altered States of Consciousness*, edited by C. Tart. Garden City, NY: Doubleday, 1972.

Stoppard, Tom. *Rosencrantz and Guildenstern Are Dead*. New York: Grove Press, 1967.

Swanton, John R. *Contributions to the Ethnology of the Haida*. New York: American Museum of Natural History, 1909.

Trungpa, Chögyam. *The Tibetan Book of the Dead*. Boulder: Shambhala, 1975.

Tzu, Lao. *The Way of Life*. Translated by Witter Bynner. New York: Capricorn, 1962.

Vass, Winifred Kelergberger. *The Bantu Speaking Heritage of the United States*. Los Angeles: Center for Afro-American Studies, UCLA, 1979.

Watts, Alan. *The Way of Zen*. New York: Vintage/Random House, 1957.

————. *The Book on the Taboo Against Knowing Who You Are*. New York: Random House, 1966.

Weiner, Annette B. "From Words to Objects to Magic: 'Hard Words' and the Boundaries of Social Interaction." In *Dangerous Words: Language and Politics in the Pacific*, edited by Donald Lawrence Brenneis and Fred R. Myers. New York: New York University Press, 1984.

Weizsäcker, Carl Friedrich von. "On the Relativity of Language." In *The Unity of Nature.* New York: Farrar, Straus Giroux, 1980.

Whorf, Benjamin Lee. *Language, Thought, and Reality.* New York: Wiley, 1956.

Witherspoon, Gary. *Language and Art in the Navajo Universe.* Ann Arbor, MI: University of Michigan Press, 1977.

Yutang, Lin. *The Importance of Living.* New York: Reynal & Hitchcock, 1938.

Zimmer, Heinrich. *Myths and Symbols in Indian Art and Civilization,* edited by Joseph Campbell. Princeton, NJ: Princeton University Press, copyright Bollingen Foundation, Washington, D.C., 1946.

KEY TO SOURCES · INDEX

If any of the words or worldviews in this book pique your interest, you might want to retrace my steps and look at some of the source material listed in the Bibliography. Although every word in this book was confirmed by referring to a dictionary of the appropriate language, several of the key words came from informants who are experts on the language in question; therefore, not all of the words are referenced to a book, an article, or a scholarly journal. The following alphabetical list includes all those words that come from linguistic studies, literary works, anthropological literature, or dictionary listings that are interesting in themselves. All bibliographic references included with these words are listed in the Bibliography.

THE AUTHOR

Howard Rheingold has written a number of works exhibiting his interest in the human mind, co-authoring such books as *Higher Creativity* and *The Cognitive Connections*. More recently his work has focused on the territory where minds meet technology, the world of artificial experience, and the cultural and political implications of the virtual community. Once Executive Editor of the magazine *HotWired*, he lives in Mill Valley, California.